Stories To Make You Smile

Coventry Writers' Group

Contents

Introduction

Coventry Writers' Group is an informal and dynamic group of writers based in and around the Coventry area.

Formed in the 1950s, the group exists to encourage and help new and established writers. We meet once a month to discuss various aspects of writing, editing and publishing, and authors often read their work aloud for discussion.

As individuals, we write in a wide variety of styles and genres. Between us, we write poetry, plays, novels, short stories, magazine articles and factual works. What links us together is a passion for writing and a love of the written word.

This is the fourth anthology that the Coventry Writers' Group has published and we decided to give it a humorous feel. Everyone needs a laugh and this book delivers. There is something for everyone from cricket stories to quiz shows, murder to mayhem, tales of ancient Troy and summer trips to the seaside.

All of our writers have risen to the challenge, so we hope you enjoy reading this anthology as much as we have enjoyed writing it.

Margaret Mather
Chairperson
Coventry Writers' Group
2017

Storm in a B Cup

by Margaret Egrot

I was eating toast and nearly didn't take the call.

"Hello?" I said eventually, still chewing and coughing slightly as a crumb caught in the back of my throat. I took a sip of tea to clear it.

"Andrea Peterson?" It was a man's voice, heavily accented, and nasal, as if he had a cold or was holding his nose. I thought he might be East European, but I'm not very good at accents.

I "uh-hu'd," in the affirmative. That, and the tea, helped shift the crumb.

"Andrea Peterson, we have your father."

There was a pause. He, presumably, to let the import of what he'd said sink in. Me because my father had been dead for over two years.

"Sorry, I think you have the wrong number." I was about to switch off, but the man cut in quickly.

"He's safe - for now. Fifty grand by the weekend or he loses a finger every day you delay. We'll be in touch."

The phone went dead. I took another mouthful of toast. It had to be a mistake. But the man – Russian, I'd decided it had to be a Russian, because this was the sort of thing Russians did in films – knew my name and my mobile phone number. Knew my new name in fact as, since the gender re-assignment surgery, I had stopped calling myself Andrew.

How had he got hold of my mobile number? Was this part of a new spate of transphobic trolling? I'd had a fair bit of that in the past few years. I scrolled through my Facebook and Twitter accounts. Nothing. So far, this call was a one off.

But the thing about chopping off Dad's fingers bothered me. Was it some kind of coded digital message? How do you chop a finger off a dead man anyway? So dead, in fact, his ashes had been deposited in an old cocoa tin on my mantelpiece whilst I decided what to do with them. I needed to agree his final resting place with my brother, who currently wasn't speaking to me. Or maybe he was – but I'd made it a rule two years ago not to open letters addressed to Andrew Peterson, and he knew that. Besides, I'd been told by an old neighbour that he had moved to a new flat and salon, but she didn't have any contact details.

I finished my toast, took three hormone boosting pills with a few swigs of my now cold tea, and rinsed the mug and plate under the hot tap.

The phone rang again. I picked up quickly this time.

"Don't phone the Police." He rang off before I had time to say a word. This time I felt the accent had a hint of Welsh, but the line went dead so quickly, I may have just imagined it. I sat looking at the phone screen – option one seemed to have been ruled out before I'd even thought of it.

The tablets always made me feel a bit queasy for a bit after I'd taken them. But it was worth it – my breasts had been growing since the start of the hormone treatment and I was a decent B cup size now. I felt them appreciatively, and for a moment they took my mind off the recent phone calls.   Then the phone rang again.

"Yes?" This time I forgot to modulate my voice in the way I'd been taught, and the word came out as a basso bark.

"Hey, steady! What's this with the macho aggression?" It was my transition mentor. I was due to see her in an hour.

"Clare, I'm sorry." I willed my voice up half an octave. "Been having a bit of bother over the phone. I thought it might be them again."

"Trannie haters?" I hated Clare using that term – in her book it seemed to cover ninety percent of the population. But I had never known how to tell her, and just now didn't feel like the right time either.

"Don't think so. It was about my Dad."

"Poor you. You think you've got them dead and buried, but there's always something still needs doing. No peace for the wicked eh?"

I glanced at the cocoa tin. For the second time in less than a minute I felt Clare's counselling skills were somewhat lacking. But she'd been through the system, well not the full bells and whistles - she'd decided to keep her bells and whistle intact - so, in the absence of any other mentors being available, I was stuck with her.

"Anyway," she went on, "I'm just ringing to say I'm running terribly behind this morning, can we leave it till the same time tomorrow? That's great. You're a star. Must dash" She rang off without waiting for a reply. I didn't believe she was too busy. More likely she had been out on a date last night and still hadn't got home. Clare never seemed short of male partners looking for something a bit different.

The phone rang again almost immediately.

"Hello?" I remembered to use my lilting contralto this time.

"About the cash. Twenty pound notes. Unmarked. In a black sports bag. We'll tell you on Thursday where to leave it."

"Hold on, I ..." But the man had rung off again. Maybe it wasn't a hint of Welsh. More Asian. Didn't parts of Eastern Europe segue into Asia Minor? I was sure Russia did, but my geography of anywhere beyond Dover was a bit shaky.

It was no use ringing Clare to discuss what I should do. I doubted very much she would pick up, and her cheery voice-mail message – "Sorry me dearies, I'm probably flat on my back somewhere. Just leave a message and I'll call you when I'm upright," delivered in a throaty coo - was more than I could stomach at the moment.

I tried talking to Dad. I even took the cocoa tin down and put it on the table next to me. At first He'd been appalled at the idea of one of his sons becoming a daughter. But after Mum died and he'd seen I was serious, he'd been surprisingly supportive. True, he'd still struggled with the fact it was his rugger playing son with a wife who'd wanted to change gender, not his first born, who had hated P.E, was a ladies' hairdresser, and still single with, what Dad would describe dismissively as 'body ishoos'. Not his only issues, I thought morosely, thinking of the frequent, and usually cruel, pranks my brother played on me when we were kids, and he was still bigger than me.

"Why couldn't you just be, um, gay?" Dad had asked me once, and I'd tried to explain. He'd gone a bit pale and cut me off with "Okay, okay! It's your decision. But I think I'll stick with the gay angle down the golf club for now." I'd never tried to discuss it with him again, but he was the one who'd given me the money for the op just before he died.

I stared hopefully at the cocoa tin, but it just sat there, impassive. Time was passing, and I could feel myself getting tense. Finally I said

"That's OK, Dad, I know you'd help me if you could," and placed the tin carefully back on the mantelpiece. As I did so, it was as if Dad had reached out to me from under the lid with one of his typically common sense suggestions.

"Of course, thanks, Dad, I'll ring her straight away." I patted the tin affectionately and dialled my ex-wife's work mobile. She may have found it impossible to stay living with a man who was now a woman, but we were still mates. And she was the best source of advice on dresses and make-up I had; Clare's style was much too flamboyant for my taste.

"Inspector Peterson."

I nearly switched off straight away. The man had told me not to call the police, and I'd forgotten that my wife always answered her mobile with her professional hat on when working, even when she knew it was me.

"Shh!" I hissed into the phone. "Don't speak so loud, Lynn, I'm in a spot of bother – no I'm not being threatened, well I am, but not how you're thinking. Look, I can't explain, we might be being listened to, but I really, really need your advice. Could you come over?"

I could picture her, checking her diary, looking at the pile of files on her desk, or smiling ruefully at a group of new constables she'd just taken responsibility for. But I was sure she'd come; she knew I never contacted her at work unless it was important. And if this didn't rate as important, what did?

Lynn sighed theatrically. "Trust you to catch me on my way to a meeting, Ands." She did her best to remember my name change, but the old one came to her first so often, we'd settled on Ands.

"Damn it! Another five minutes and I'd have switched this blasted thing off, and missed you. OK, I'll just find someone to cover for me, and I'll be with you in an hour. Get the kettle on."

I nearly wet myself with relief.

"Thank you. You're a pal! Just one thing –

please don't come in your uniform, or in a force car."

"But...? Oh all right. You can explain when I get to you. I'll go home first, but that'll add another twenty minutes." I caught the start of another heavy sigh as she switched her phone off.

I glanced at the cocoa tin. Was it such a good idea after all? The man hadn't said I wasn't to use my phone, only not to ring the police. So an ex-wife shouldn't count. But an ex-wife who was a police officer? One who had spent time in a specialist unit dealing with abduction and ransom negotiations? Wouldn't that count as contacting the Police? I started to sweat.

But how would they find out? Were they tapping my phone, and would they now know the police – in the guise of my ex-wife – were already on their way? Were they watching the flat and would they intercept her on her way in? Was I putting her and Dad in danger? Oh God, had I just done something really, really, stupid? I glanced at the cocoa tin for guidance and very nearly burst out laughing. Of course Dad wasn't in danger.

The mirror over the mantelpiece showed my reflection from the waist up. A quite good looking, if rather well built, woman stared back at me. I was still in my nightie and dressing gown, and my hair needed combing. I'd had it dyed, but I wasn't sure about the colour and my roots were showing through. Lynn, who was allowing herself to go grey naturally, and whose care regime, even when we were married, seemed to consist of nothing more than a trim every six weeks, had been no use when it came to female hair fashion. My brother would have been able to advise me. But I'd have hair down to the waist by now, if I'd waited for him to come round. I rubbed my chin and realised that, whilst five o'clock shadow was a thing of the past, early morning stubble was not. My legs probably needed shaving too.

I had over an hour before Lynn was due to arrive which gave me plenty of time to get myself ready. I'd already settled on wearing one of the skirt and blouse sets she had chosen with me a couple of weeks ago. She would like that – at least she would prefer it to seeing me unshaven and still in a nightie. I headed for the bathroom. After a moment's hesitation, I went back to collect the phone.

One of the very few things I haven't liked about my life as a woman, so far, is having to sit down for a pee. It takes up so much time compared with the quick point and shake I'd been used to. On the other hand, it was easier to take a phone call from a sedentary position. I merely had to reach out a hand, and take my mobile from the side of the bath, when it rang.

"Your dad needs his medication, He's not looking too good. We want the money in two days."

I felt sorry for the poor man, whoever it was they'd got. But what was I supposed to do about it?

"He's not my …." I started, but the man cut in:

"Just get us the bloody money. Right?" and rang off. I stared at the phone to confirm the call had ended, and put it back on the edge of the bath. When finished, I stood up and flushed the toilet. I was puzzled. This time, the still nasally East European voice had taken on a decidedly Brummie whine. An accent I knew well – I had the same myself.

****

Lynn arrived in under an hour. She'd obviously picked up on my anxiety and come as quickly as she could. I could have kissed her, but knew she would back away; sisterly camaraderie she could just about cope with, physical displays of affection were too much of a reminder of the husband she'd lost.

As I was closing the door behind her I realised that I should have checked first, before swooping down the hall to let her in. What if it had been the kidnappers? I hastily ushered her further down the hall and re-opened the front door just wide enough to poke my head out, to see if she had been followed. The road looked empty.

"Gosh, Ands, you are in a state. Get me that tea and tell me more." Her presence, as always, calmed me down.

Over two mugs of tea and several Rich Tea biscuits (I'd no idea you could be so hungry when so anxious) I told her everything. She took notes and nodded several times as I spoke, but didn't interject. Police training I suppose.

"Do you think I ought to tell Kevin?" I asked as I finished.

"Idiot. Your brother already knows that your dad is dead," She replied.

She was silent for a long time, and I could see that she was thinking.

"Did you check the number that rang?" she said eventually.

"Yes. Number withheld."

"Mind if I take a look?"

She took my phone and fiddled round for several minutes, as I looked on uncomprehendingly. Suddenly a number came up on the screen.

"But …"

"Don't ask. Trade secret." She winked, then added, "I suppose that's why your caller said don't contact the police."

The calls had been from a landline, with a

Birmingham code, but I didn't recognise the number. None-the-less, it felt like a big step forward. I felt a warm glow of gratitude sweep through me and, with difficulty, I stopped myself from giving her a hug.

"What now?" I asked instead, my hands clasped round my mug.

Lynn shrugged. Then a look came over her face – a look I knew only too well: she'd had an idea. She reached into her bag and took out a mobile. It wasn't her work one and I hadn't seen it before. One glance from her told me that this was private and personal, and none of my business. True - but was still disconcerting to be reminded that she too had a new life now.

"Just a minute."

Using her new phone, she dialled the number displayed on my screen. After a few rings the call was answered.

"Oh hallo, I wonder if you could fit me in for a trim today? Great! I'm on my lunch break, any chance of something within the next half hour? 1.30? That would be awesome. My name? Oh, umm, Hilary. No, just the one 'l'. The man's spelling? If you say so! Oh, remind me - where exactly is the salon?" She scribbled something down. "Thank you so much, I'll see you soon."

I glared at her. At a time like this why was Lynn, of all people, taking time out to book a hair appointment? Wasn't tracking down my caller more important?

She looked up at me, a triumphant smile breaking through.

"Oh, Ands, your face is a picture! That was Kevin's new salon. Seems like your brother wants to get in touch with you after all. It's just like him not to make it straightforward. Come on, we'll go to my place so I can put my uniform back on before we see him. Personally I think my hair's just fine, but he's got a bit of explaining to do, and a slight fright from the long arm of the law won't do him any harm at all."

Kevin? No wonder the voice had started to sound familiar!

Whilst Lynn used the bathroom, I ran a finger under my bra to settle my breasts more comfortably into their cups, and checked my make-up and hair in the over-mantel mirror. All seemed fine. I put on a jacket, and picked up my handbag and the front door keys.

"Ready?" said Lynn as she came back into the living room. I nodded and followed her down the hall. I couldn't help grinning at the thought that I'd got the better of my brother for once, even if it was my ex-wife who'd done it really.

As we got to the front door, a thought came to me.

"Just a moment."

I ran back into the living room, took the cocoa tin down from the mantelpiece, and placed it carefully in my handbag. Dad wouldn't want to miss out on a family re-union like this.

The surprisingly long death of Edward Breslin

by John Sutton

Edward Breslin had lived a reasonably happy life for his 50 odd years. Admittedly, people who saw the Harley-Davidson motorbike, and particularly those who heard his old nickname ("The Barracuda") tended to get the wrong idea about him, but the truth was that he got the nickname while fishing on holiday. He hadn't fished in salt water before, and was hoping to get something a few inches long with interesting colours. Instead, he got this 4 feet long monstrosity with a mouth full of razor sharp fangs, which nearly dragged him in. He'd almost been put off fishing for life by that, and no-one had stopped ribbing him about it since. It'd been a long time since he left the old biking club, and he couldn't really remember why, but he was fairly certain that their insistence on calling him that was one of the reasons, maybe one of the major ones.

A lot had changed since then. Most of his friends were in that biking club, so without much peer pressure to hold him back, he'd rather let himself go. Nowadays almost no-one would call him "The Barracuda". More likely it'd be "The Water Balloon". He was almost a comical sight on the bike nowadays, but he didn't care. He loved that bike, he loved the look of it, the feel of it, even the smell of it. He'd keep riding that bike around for the pleasure of it till the day he died. Literally.

On that fateful day, he was riding it around the outer ring road, and he was enjoying himself thoroughly. He was still some distance from the next junction when the lights turned green. There were only a few vehicles at the light, and they started pulling out almost immediately, so he wouldn't even need to slow down. He could keep on cruising, just the way he liked it.

What no-one there knew (yet) was that a particularly awkwardly placed burst water main had been slowly leaking water right under the junction for most of the winter. The road was quite well made, but with repeated freezes and thaws throughout the whole winter, it was only a matter of time till a pothole formed. Most potholes were only one or two feet across, and a few inches deep, but then, most pothole formation didn't involve the whole road steadily disintegrating.

As Edward approached the junction, he saw a coach approaching the junction from the left. By all rights, even with no traffic in front of it, it should have stopped for the red light, but the driver was running badly late, and had slept poorly. He wasn't paying enough attention to the road, and started to brake a bit too late. Ironically, though, it wasn't the coach that finally broke through the damaged road. By sheer, blind bad luck, it was a white truck only a few places in front of Edward that drove over one of the thinnest parts of the junction. With plenty of vehicles already crossing, the road surface simply couldn't take it any longer. The existing cracks quickly grew, further reducing the roads ability to take the strain, until finally it all gave way.

Suddenly, all the vehicles weren't driving across smooth, flat road, but collapsing into a hole some two feet deep and nearly 20 feet across. The bottom was flat enough to avoid sending any vehicles tumbling over, but with a lip that steep and high, everyone knew it would catch the wheels of most vehicles trying to cross it, which would almost certainly flip the vehicle. Everyone immediately tried an emergency stop. The result was inevitable, a huge pile-up, worse than any that had happened there in decades.

Edward knew he was too close to the car in front to stop in time, and steered round it instead, but then the driver of the next car noticed the coach, and desperately went into a turn to stop him(her?)self going into the hole. With no chance of dodging it, the bike hit the side of the car at nearly 40 miles an hour, and Edward went flying straight over the bonnet of the car. At the same time, the coach (which was still well over the speed limit) clipped a van and went out of control, twisting sideways and going into a roll.

Edward, for his part, soon realised he was on a collision course with the rear end of the (soon to be sideways) coach. He knew what that meant. He'd be splattered like a bug on a windshield. He was still in midair, had no way to dodge it. He was going to die, wasn't he?

The moment he realised that, everything suddenly stopped. Panicked drivers froze up, midscream. Cars and trucks and bikes, no matter how fast they were going two seconds ago, just... didn't move, as if Edward was stuck inside a photograph. Even he was stuck there, just hanging in mid-air. It was so bizarre that he couldn't take it in, at first. He tried to turn his head, tried to see what was happening, but he couldn't move any more than anyone else could. He tried to shut it out, to close his eyes and wait to die, but he couldn't even move his eyelids. Slowly, a cold, hard fact sunk in. He was well and truly stuck there. He didn't understand how this could possibly have happened, but the fact was, now it had happened, he was lumbered with it. He wondered what he could do to pass the time while he waited for whatever it was to end. But then, he realised – he might not be able to move his head, but from here, he had a surprisingly good view of the road, all the vehicles, all the drivers. He wouldn't even have noticed them if the accident hadn't happened, but now he had all the time in the world to study them, see if he recognised anyone, try to work out who would live, and who would die. Maybe he'd even figure out how this had happened.

The first driver he noticed was in the middle of screaming in fury at the driver in front, apparently blaming him. It was a ridiculous sentiment – no one person was to blame for all of this, it was just too big. Even the coach driver, presumably a bit of an idiot, couldn't have predicted a failure of this magnitude. Certainly one random driver wasn't significantly to blame. The furious driver was just being foolish. He wasn't anything interesting.

Then he noticed someone riding a bike. Not his sort, the non-motorized variety. At first, he wanted to laugh, but then he realised the bike owner would avoid all of this easily. It was too slow, too easy to stop for a road accident (even one this big) to be a problem. Edward was briefly jealous, annoyed that his beloved bike had a part in his death (assuming his death was still going to happen). He couldn't stay annoyed at it though. It was just too important to him. On the other hand, the driver of that damned car that turned into his path might as well be an incarnation of the devil. That driver wasn't just killing him, he'd damaged the bike. He'd never wanted anyone to die before, but he did now. Worse, he wanted it to be slow and excruciatingly painful.

But then he caught himself. He wasn't that kind of man. He'd been part of a club once, not a gang. It was a proper, government-sanctioned club that existed to make sure all its members followed all the relevant laws and safety regulations that existed to stop an open air two wheeled high speed road vehicle from turning into a death trap. Not that they had helped much here. The turning driver wasn't some vicious murderer out to destroy his life and ruin his beloved bike, he (or perhaps she? It wasn't like he could turn his head to check) was just desperate. Maybe (s)he cared just as much about the car as he did about his bike. Suddenly sympathetic and guilt ridden, Edward silently apologised. It was pointless, really. The driver didn't know, couldn't even see Edward.

They were both stuck in exactly the same spot as before, after all.

Or were they?

He'd paid plenty of attention to the coach when he first went flying, but he could swear it was just a hint closer. He paid more attention to the nearest vehicle, in front and to one side. It was maybe a fraction of an inch closer than it had been when things had first frozen, some 25 apparent seconds ago. His maths skills weren't up to the job of working out how much "real time" had passed, and he didn't have accurate enough numbers to work it out even if he did have the skills, but the implication was clear. Time hadn't stopped. It had just slowed down, everything except his ability to think. It was an odd thing to make an exception for – he thought that thinking was just electrical impulses running through his brain. Why would they be any different from electrical impulses running through his nervous system trying to get him to move? It didn't make any sense. Still, it did mean his end was still coming. It was taking rather longer than expected, that was all...

Now he knew that he could still move, he set to the task of turning his eyes in a different direction. It was painfully slow work (so slow he hadn't even noticed the movement when he tried earlier), but his view slowly crawled across. Once his capacity for movement was confirmed, he started looking for signs of it in other drivers. One random stranger after another was just terrified, but then he saw one driver, heading straight for her doom just as most of them were, but with a look of utter bewilderment on her face. He imagined that look on his own face just after everything froze. It was the same, she was still trying to figure out what was happening. He wasn't the only one who could think!

He was fine with standing out in a crowd for most things, but this was so weird he was relieved not to be alone. Now he just had to use his remaining time to work out how this was happening.

It took another minute or two for him to catch on. What happens just before you die? Your life flashes before your eyes. How long would it take a clip show of nearly 50 years of life to flick in front of you? Far too long for an accident like this. Presumably, then, time (or at least your own view of it) warped to give you enough time to remember it all. Obviously something had gone wrong here, because the time warp had kicked in but the flashbacks hadn't. Maybe too many people were about to die? Maybe the system overloaded somehow?

Pleased with himself that he'd managed to figure it out, he started looking at the female driver, tried to shift his expression to say "don't worry, it'll all be done soon". He wasn't sure how well it worked (it wasn't like he had a mirror to check), but he was already well on his way to hitting the coach now. He didn't have time to wait for her to show her reaction, he needed to know if anyone he knew was here. He hoped it worked, though, that he'd given a bit of comfort to someone in need in his last moments.

He checked the pedestrians first. There wasn't anyone he knew among them, but there were a few people of interest. One woman with a pushchair had only narrowly avoided pushing it into the hole. One man was so shocked at the accident he was halfway through fainting. One passing blogger seemed excited it was happening (she'd already turned her camera on the scene).

It took a while to spot and recognise Alan. Poor old Alan "Meathook" Richards, one of his old comrades. They hadn't met in twenty years. He'd got the nickname as a child, since his father was a butcher and they didn't have a swing. Predictably, Alan had improvised. He wondered if any of the old bikers got these nicknames the way people assumed they had...

Mercifully, Alan (in a car, with a family!) was far back enough to avoid the whole crash. Of course, that meant the timewarp hadn't kicked in for him. No flicker of confusion in his eyes, just alarm. That meant he almost certainly wouldn't notice and recognise Edward in time, so they wouldn't have one more meeting before he died. It was a shame, but at least Alan and his family were safe.

Edward looked for someone else he knew, but after several minutes, he realised. There was noone else he knew. So much for that way to pass the time. What was he supposed to do now? Study the pigeon flying out of a tree in a panic? Stupid bird, nothing was going to hit the tree. Study the road, try to work out how such a huge pothole had opened? He'd never seen one over a foot or two across before. He didn't know enough about how potholes opened, and it wasn't like he had a convenient library in his head to check. He couldn't begin to guess. Writing a will in his head was pointless as well, since no-one would ever see it, and he didn't have anyone to give his stuff to, anyway. He was an only child, and his parents were long dead.

So what could he do? There was nothing, as far as he could tell. Would he just have to hang here, getting more bored by the minute, until it finally happened? Not if he could help it. There was a good reason he never travelled except by bike. He didn't get bored on the bike, and he knew what happened when he got bored. He always started to nod off, which was exactly what he didn't want to happen on a bus or train. The risk of missing his stop was too high. Now, though, he welcomed it. Some people wanted to go out with a bang, to jump into a live volcano instead of die of cancer. Not Edward. He'd always wanted to die peacefully, sleeping in his own bed, surrounded by family and friends. He couldn't have his bed now, of course, but he could have his last, good, deep sleep. Alan almost counted as family, too, despite all that time that had passed. Two out of three wasn't bad.

His eyes finally finished closing, and Edward slowly drifted off. Maybe the time warp wasn't so bad after all. Everyone died in the end, but the warp had turned a terrible, painful death into a nice, gentle one. Maybe that was the point?

Edward himself never felt the impact of the coach, but several survivors of the catastrophe reported a truly bizarre sight – a huge, overweight man asleep and snoring in mid air just before he died. The blogger even managed to get some footage of it, which quickly showed up (as a photo) in the local papers. Several of his old friends saw it, and Edwards funeral had a rather bigger crowd than he expected.

The headstone said "If you're going to die, you might as well be doing something you enjoy when it happens".

Pension Crisis

by Charles Satchwell

George was sixty-nine. He still played tennis and walked his dog twice a day. He wasn't overweight, had never smoked and only drank in moderation. Getting up at the usual hour he didn't feel his normal chirpy self. As he sat down at the kitchen table he told his wife he felt strange. A few minutes later his head flopped forward into his bowl of porridge. His wife, unable to locate a pulse, called 999 and left him still slumped in the gooey mess. While waiting for the ambulance to arrive she decided to attempt mouth to mouth resuscitation by lifting his head by his hair and blowing into his mouth. It was a futile attempt to revive him. She wiped her hands on her apron, licked porridge from her lips, and thought that it was much too sweet for her liking. The paramedics came and placed him in the recovery position, his face was covered in porridge. They pumped hard on his chest but it was no good, George had eaten his last bowl of oats. The paramedic, who seemed the more sympathetic of the two, stood up, shaking his head in dismay.

"It would be better to clean him up a little before we put him in the ambulance. Have you got a flannel to wipe his face?"

"Of course."

George's wife ran into the kitchen and returned with a dish cloth. She wiped his face like he was a child who was a messy eater. As she studied his tranquil expression a tear appeared in her eye. She was devastated. Porridge was his favourite. There was nothing he liked better than to start the day with a hot bowl of oats laced with honey and she'd made it extra thick today. What a waste!

Life expectancy had risen to eighty-nine for men and ninety-four for women. Consequently, British citizens didn't receive the state pension until reaching the ripe old age of sixty-eight years of age. The civil servants, sitting around the solid, mahogany, board room table, all seemed to have the same pensive look on their faces as they scrutinized the documents laid out in front of them. The six men that made up the committee knew that the destiny of the residents of their beloved country was in their hands. The target figures had been met and the outcome was having the desired effect on the population, everything seemed to be going according to plan. The media had not reported anything suspicious and the general public didn't have an inkling that anything was amiss. The Chairman took a few more minutes to collect his thoughts before he stood up. The room was silent, all eyes focused on him, as he pushed his reading glasses back over his nose and started to speak.

"One year ago, in this very room, we took an incredible decision which was life changing in every sense of the words. We are all aware of the seriousness of the situation and I believe that the conclusion we came to was the correct one. I trust that the age we settled on for the data base was as it should be. Are we all happy with the arrangements?"

A thin middle-aged man raised his hand and all eyes focused on him.

"Mr. Chairman, I know that we discussed exemptions last year but I feel that we should revisit this area of the operation."

"Out of the question. We spent an interminable amount of time discussing exemptions and it was unanimously decided that there cannot be any. It must contain everyone over the age of sixty-five years, without exception. We can, of course, review the starting age, as sixty-six was narrowly defeated in the vote."

"Surely priests and civil servants should be exempt?"

"I repeat for the last time we are not going to discuss any exceptions to the universal makeup of the data base. We are here to review whether the pilot has been successful. I believe that five hundred a week, approximately twenty-six thousand this year, is going to alleviate our problems in the long run. If not we can always increase the weekly amount, but I believe that we should stay with five hundred a week for at least the next twelve months when we will meet again to revisit the whole operation."

William had been doing the job for twelve months and this assignment was proving to be a little tricky. Of course, no two were the same, some were easy while others were more problematic. The woman left work at her normal time and dashed to her car. She always seemed to be in a hurry and drove off before he could even think about intercepting her. William followed, keeping his distance so as not to arouse suspicion. Eventually she parked on the drive of her semi-detached house in the suburbs. From her profile, he knew that her name was Sally, she was sixty-five, married, with two grown up sons who had both flown the nest. She worked for a large insurance company. It was unusual to get someone who was still working. Most of his assignments were elderly, retired, ladies or gentlemen. From previous surveillance, he surmised that she was unlikely to emerge from her home this evening. He could see the light from the wide screen television through the gap in the curtains. The television stayed on until about 10.30 pm when the bedroom light went on. William settled down for another night sleeping in the car. He hoped to be ready and waiting when she came out in the morning.

The Chairman thought back to the fateful day that they made the most important decision in the history of mankind, reassuring himself that they had no alternative. They had checked and double checked the figures and it had to be done. The government was facing a financial crisis. Pension funds had gone bankrupt due to the ever-increasing duration of people's lives. The government would eventually not be able to afford to give a pension to everyone aged over sixty-eight and the cost to the national health service of the elderly was staggering.

Initially the committee's preference was to put a cap on the age to which people should live, eighty-five was the popular choice. It did seem much the fairest way of doing things. One of the most respected of the esteemed assembly had put it rather aptly.

"Eighty-five is rather a good innings. One could hardly complain about being given out after such a good knock."

The gentleman's love for cricket seemed to permeate all his comments nowadays. But it was decided that a cap would alert suspicions, so it was eventually abandoned.

William was still dozing when he heard the front door open and close. This was the second time. On the first occasion, it was Sally's husband going to work but this time she emerged wearing a tailored jacket and pleated dress. He felt his wrist for his watch but it wasn't there. He remembered that he'd put it in the glove compartment to be on the safe side. Carefully he lifted it out and put it on his wrist. Looking through the windscreen he realized that he was too late as she was already starting up the car. He punched the steering wheel in frustration. As she drove off William switched on the radio to calm his mind before turning the key in the ignition and following her. Next time he would be ready when the opportunity presented itself.

The committee members realised that if everyone reaching the age of eighty-five suddenly died, someone was bound to notice the coincidence. As soon as the media got wind there would be hell to pay. Questions would be raised in parliament and the game would be up. The public could not be trusted. They would never accept the inevitable, logical conclusion of the cull. It was the duty of the men of destiny, the cream of those chosen, to make challenging decisions and hard choices. To achieve the desired, effect the only acceptable solution was to make it more random. The names of everyone over the age of sixty-five were selected for the data base and assigned a number. Every week RASP (the computer's random allocation selection programme) selected five hundred numbers. Control converted the numbers back to names and produced dossiers of the chosen individuals. These were dispatched to disposal agents located all over the country. The agents employed had been carefully chosen, briefed and sworn to secrecy. There was a rumour gong around the table that the British model was being contemplated in other countries. This worried the chairman as it meant there might be a leak, but it did, at least, indicate that they had got things right.

William had lots of time to think in this job. In that respect, it was probably the best occupation he'd ever had. Two assignments a week meant that he could take his time and do the job properly. If he got finished early he could apply for overtime, knowing that Control was often amenable to extra assignments. The pay was okay but overtime was a big help.

He knew where she worked so he decided to overtake her and get there first to position himself appropriately. The old 'drop a scarf' routine worked best with women. He just needed to be in the right place to intercept her after she parked her car and walked to her office. Being a disposal agent, or terminator as he liked to think of himself, is not an easy profession. The difficulty is doing it without arousing suspicion. The modus operandi used before the development of the new poison were varied and hap hazard. Hit and run had been popular but it was problematic with all the surveillance cameras around. Even though the police were pressured from up high not to follow up on the case. The invention of the slow acting, but deadly, poison made the terminator's job a lot easier. You only needed a few drops and it was almost impossible to trace afterwards. Stick the victim, or client as William preferred to call them, when he, or she, wasn't looking then hit the road. Twelve hours later they dropped dead and you were long gone. His last assignment was a doddle. Stuck old George in the pub with a friendly pat on the back. A few phone calls later and William knew for certain he'd had a result. He put on his special glove, quickly climbed out of the car, and ran up to the woman.

"Excuse me, love. I think you dropped this."

As she turned around William was bending down behind her. He stood up, stretched out his hand, and offered her the scarf. As she attempted to take it he accidentally dropped it and they both bent down together to retrieve it. William let her get to the scarf first and waited as she inspected it.

"This isn't mine."

Before she stood up William pressed the button hidden in the palm of his special glove and a spike popped out of the buckle in his watch strap. He stuck it in her neck. She felt the prick and put a hand to her face, looking at him with suspicion in her eyes.

"What was that?"

"You must have rubbed up against the sharp edge of my broken badge."

William touched a fake, metal, security badge that he was wearing on his jacket lapel. She frowned at him.

"This is definitely not my scarf."

"Oh, I thought you must have dropped it when you got out of your car."

"You must be mistaken."

"I'm sorry to have bothered you, love."

William took back the scarf and, surreptitiously, pushed the button in his glove and the spike retracted. He turned around and walked back to his car. The woman stood for a while with a bemused look on her face before continuing into her office. This would be her last working day. Another unexplained heart attack.

ABC Quiz Hero

by Beverley Woodley

I still can't believe this is happening to me. When the pleasant sounding journalist called and asked if I'd do an interview about meeting my hero - I never thought it would take place in such a plush London hotel. My gaze falls on the pristine white linen on the table in front of me. I smile at the tiny sandwiches and patisserie style cakes invitingly displayed on three tiers of bone china plates. I've wanted to have afternoon tea at a swanky hotel for so long, but could never justify the expense – there was always something more sensible I had to spend the money on. Well, that's something I don't have to worry about now.

The journalist is really friendly and I feel like I'm talking to an old friend rather than being interviewed. So, I've decided she deserves the true story. Taking a deep breath I start at the beginning.

I recall how nervous and excited I was when our John persuaded me to apply to go on the show.

"You'll be great, Mum," he said. "You love that quiz and they're holding local auditions next week."

I still wasn't sure, but he knew exactly what to say to get me to go. He quoted his Dad, my late husband, "You only live once. So, live your dream and don't end up full of regrets."

I must admit, the local auditions were fun. Obviously, I didn't know how these things worked. In my naivety, I thought I'd meet Kay Meek - the host of the show but she wasn't there. Kay was the main reason why I loved the show so much. I thought she was a wonderful role model for women – my hero.

There was a real cross-section of people and age groups at the audition. A few 'show offs', but on the whole everyone was nice and friendly. They nicknamed me Goldie. It made me chuckle. I'd had some blonde foils put in to hide my grey and now I'd got a nickname. I felt young again. What a lovely bunch. In fact I'm still in touch with a few of them. We all got our turn at being contestants and a polite young man called Dave acted as the host. I felt like I was at a local amateur dramatics group. You know, doing a play about a quiz show with a group of friends. I was disappointed I hadn't met Kay, but it was all very exciting and I had a wonderful day out.

A few weeks later the letter arrived. I'd been selected! Not only that, but the TV company would pay my travel expenses to get me to the studio. I couldn't wait to get into the office and book the time off. In the evening, after work, I bought myself a whole new outfit including some nice navy court shoes. Mind you, I made sure they would be suitable for work afterwards - Waste not want not as they say.

If only I'd known how long it took to film a one hour show. I'd definitely have bought flat shoes! Oh, how my feet ached. I remember checking my watch. Nearly three hours I'd been there and they'd stopped filming again. Well, at least I now know the best remedy for nerves – boredom.

I'd been watching the stagehands setting up the final head-to-head. They were like ants on a mission carrying their heavy loads. No not ants, they were worker bees - dancing to the Queen Bee's tune. I shifted my gaze to the Queen Bee herself - the quiz show host.

They say, never meet your heroes. Well, Kay, 'Quiz Host of the Year' Meek was anything but Meek! I looked at her, resplendent in her designer suit as she alternated between ordering her hairdresser to tame invisible stray hairs and belittling her make-up artist.

I felt disappointed and let down. Kay may have thought her 'joke' in the initial round about my supermarket outfit was funny, but I'd like to think I'm not so shallow as to take offence about my appearance. It's what's on the inside that counts - not how one looks externally.

I'm still a bit annoyed about the way Kay practically ignored me and the older gentleman in the early rounds. In every break she flirted outrageously with the young male contestants...until they'd slowly been eliminated leaving, well, leaving just little old me.

Kay's make-up artist rushed past me and whispered in passing, "Sorry, I don't have time to touch up your make-up. They're about to start filming."

"That's okay, Love." I smiled.

"In Three... Two... One..."

"Welcome back and congratulations on making it this far." Kay's face oozed sincerity down the camera lens. She completely avoided looking at me.

"As our regular viewers know, twenty-six answers will be displayed on the board labelled A to Z. You'll have sixty seconds to memorise them. Then the answers will disappear. You'll be left with just the alphabet. I'll ask a question. To win the UK's largest ABC Jackpot, all you need to do is give me the letter the correct answer is hiding behind. Are you ready?"

I nodded.

"Your ABC time starts...now!"

Not even a 'Good luck'? She always says, 'Good Luck' - or maybe she only says that to the young men. She was certainly very chatty to them earlier. She obviously wasn't interested in a mature contestant like me. I used to be a huge Kay Meek fan, but not now...

"Half your time has gone."

I tried to concentrate. 'A' equals 'Phobia', 'B'

equals 'The Great Wall of China', 'C' equals... but what was the point? Meeting my hero had been such a disappointment. At that moment part of me wished I'd never got through the local auditions. I met some great people there and had a fantastic day out. I know people in real life aren't always the same as they are portrayed in the media but... Damn! My mind had drifted off again. 'C' equals ...

"Times up! So, for the UK's highest jackpot, and remember I have to take your first answer, what is the square root of nine?"

So, there I was, about to make a fool of myself on national telly. The last time I was at school the square root of nine wasn't 'Phobia' or 'The Great Wall of China'! Pick any letter and wait for the audience to have a good laugh. What should I choose?

"I have to hurry you."

"The answer is...Oh, Kay," I'd decided to confess. You know how it is. I was brought up to believe honesty is always the best policy. However, 'Little Miss Interruption' didn't wait for me to finish. I was going to say, 'Oh, Kay, I'll have to guess.' I never got the chance. Kay, staying consistent to the end, cut me short one last time.

"You said 'O', the answer is..."

Picking up my cup of tea, I look the interviewer straight in the eye, "...and that's the true story behind how I became the first ABC Quiz millionaire."

Eclipse an

On an ugly hour of the mornii
single decker bus. We were go
was Easter Monday.

On the coach, all the
around the weather. If you t(
true, it had poured down w   past
hundred years on that date. The forecast for this late
April day promised warmth and sunshine.

Dad still had a gripe about what it cost him last
year in 1956. We were forced to shelter from the rain
in a penny arcade. He reckoned paying off the national
debt would have been cheaper than feeding us boys
with coins for playing the machines.

My older brother Tom, said if Dad did a bit more
overtime, he would not have to be so mean to his
children.

Father went into a rant and reeled off everything
he had bought Tom since his birth. From the first pair
of nappies, through to the television so we could
watch the Queen's Coronation, to the 11th birthday
gift of a telescope.

That telescope was Tom's great obsession, next
to football. Because of his interest in the cosmos,
Mum let him stay up late and watch 'The Sky at
Night.' A brand new programme to Television. I did
not think the show had legs to run for long. What
viewer would want to see a scrag dressed bloke, with
a monocle, who talked faster than a firing machine
gun. Anyway I got packed off to bed before it was on,
which, at the time, seemed not at all fair.

Mum opened her just in case bag. She had
taken out the first pack of sandwiches of the day.
Each member of the family got a bacon doorstep. The

ad bestowed the desired effect on
up.
ied, Mum's just in case bag held anything
be needed for a day out. The only thing
was alcohol. Mum came from a family that
bible reading and strictly teetotal. Dad, in
contrast, grew up in a culture that would celebrate 'no drinking day' with a dram of whisky. If Scott of the Antarctic had Mum's holdall he would have got back from the South Pole.

The coach reached the seaside destination and disgorged its passengers. As a herd, the day trippers raced to the beach. There we took up squatters rights. Dad hired a couple of deck chairs. Tom and I had to sit on the sand.

After a full two minutes, Tom was bored. He wished to be back home. Brother wanted the company of his mates. Dad held no truck to these moans and groans. Tom got told to cheer up or clear off.

Brother walked off in a huff. Dad said he will be glad when the grump reaches his teens. With a bit of luck, Tom would not speak to the rest of the family for a good seven years.

Tom did not go too far away. He came across a gang of big boys playing football. They let him join their game. My brother was occupied for the rest of that day.

I stripped off to my swim trunks. Thanks to Mum's forethought, I had put them on before leaving home. It saved the embarrassment of trying to change under a towel. Always at the critical moment the covering would fall off. Mind it was a great hoot when this happened to someone else.

I ran down the beach and charged into the waves. The shock of the cold took my breath away. Those waters were iceberg freezing. The sun had lied by giving the sea a glowing shimmer. It was only an illusion of warmth. I escaped this melt glacial environ with the panic of a naked Eskimo chased by a polar bear.

In my haste to be clear of the water I stumbled over. Sand castles were sent flying and destroyed. This put the builder into a screaming rage. She whacked me with the flat of her spade. My foe was a fair haired girl. We were both about the same height.

With the cold of the sea chilling me to the marrow, the pain of my arm being shown up as a purple bruise, I was gritted up for some pigtail pulling. I heard my name "Cyan". It was the calm voice of Mum. She had brought my bucket and spade. Mum asked the girl her name. Eclipse came the reply. She was given a small chocolate bar as compensation for the wreckage of the sand castles. On promising to help repair the damage caused, I was also given the same treat.

The pain in my arm eased off and the heat of the sun took away the sea chill. To build sand castles with Eclipse seemed to be a good idea.

Some time later a Nordic looking man came up and gave us each a cornet. Eclipse explained that was her father. Licking the ice cream I thought she was a girl worth knowing.

The tide ebbed out. The best castles were made from damp sand. We moved to always be on that wet band of beach, newly gained from the sea. A line of castles showed our progress, from the high tide mark to a continually receding waterline.

Dad came on a brief visit. He gave us both a bottle of orangeade. Eclipse taught me how to gulp down the fizzy drink at speed, so you could then exude a loud burp. When I went back to school my pals thought it a great wheeze. Mum was not amused.

My new friend told me she was born in Nigeria,

in 1951, during a total eclipse of the sun. The girl's skin was paler than mine. That did not seem right. People who come from Africa were black. She claimed the reason was obvious. On the day of her birth the sun did not shine.

I said my birthday happened in the same September as her's. On the first day of my life the sun had shone blue. That is why my name is Cyan.

Big brother once told me I had a squeak close escape from a lifetime of having fun poked at me. His name came from Dad's dad, Grandpa Thomas. Mum's father expected the same honour to be bestowed on him, if another child was born. The trouble was he had a rambling biblical name that was no longer in vogue. Even worse than that, in its line of letters a person could read one of the rudest words in the English language.   Luckily the expletive did not come out when spoken.

Mum considered it bad enough to have the word written on her birth certificate. She would not relay the snigger factor onto her own child.

By the dint of good luck, the strange event of a blue sun gave Mum a great reason not to name me after her father. To placate his injured pride, my parents vowed the next baby would be named after him. If the infant was female they would girlify the name.

Mum and Dad held no intention of having a larger family. I agreed with them on that. It was bad enough having to share with an older brother. Anyway who would want more children once they had me.

That beach became the realm of our imagination. Everyday objects took on magic forms. Ordinary people became characters out of picture books.

Dad turned up again. He had bought a box of miniature flags from a nearby souvenir shop.

They were made from paper and cocktail sticks. We put them on the top of our castles. These pennons smelt of being old stock. The packaging had "League of Nation Flags" printed on it, with the date 1937. One flag was a swastika. I hoped Mum had Dad's war medals in her bag. Just in case someone took offence.

The old man left us and went further along the beach. He joined in with the football match. I am sure that annoyed Tom. To niggle my brother further, Dad played on the opposing side. I can hear Tom now, complaining Father had took part just to show him up.

Dad was not the only adult to be in the game. For such an ancient creature, he was an able footballer. There were players his age in the proper professional soccer league.

I observed Dad, along with the other oldies, played more of a long passing game. While the younger ones, despite what team they were in, followed the ball as a swarm.

After one tackle, Dad took control of the ball. The only person able to stop him scoring was number one son. Tom came in close to block the way. Father grabbed the lad and threw him across his shoulder. As he carried the struggling boy, Dad dribbled the ball into the open goal mouth.

A loud cheer erupted from the winning team. Dad dumped Tom on the sand. In frustration my brother screamed it was a foul. Father raised a clenched fist in triumph, then left the pitch.

A black beast strode the beach. His intent was to destroy our city of flags. We tried to scare him off. He charged in. Eclipse attempted to hold him by his neck. She got badly licked with a rough tongue. I grabbed the fur on his back. The beast had more strength than me. My body got dragged around. Sand flew all over the place.

An out of breath fat Ogre came running up in

swim trunks. He called the beast a naughty Fido, put a lead on his collar, then walked off with him.

We set about repairing the ravages of battle. Some castles were abandoned to remain as ruins, just like the bomb sites back in my home town. The sea was in retreat no more.

After a glorious long day the tide turned and began to advance up the beach. One by one the castles we had built were dissolved by the surf. The water rolled over the sand to lay it pristine flat. All our efforts looked as if they had never been. The sun that had won the day with the clouds started to fall from the sky, to be doused at the far rim of the sea.

I heard my Mum's voice. She told me it was time to leave the beach.

Dad had gone to pull Tom out of the football game. I imagined some of those boys would still be playing in the midnight moonlight.

The family ambled back to the coach park. As fate would have it, Eclipse and her parents were going in the same direction. Because of Mum's concern about missing the bus, we arrived far too early. The drivers had not yet returned, the coaches were locked.

Our family were not the only ones to turn up so early. We became part of an ever growing crowd. Mum was getting an earful from Tom. He, at the slightest quiver in her resolve, would have ran back to the never ending game of football.

Dad had got chatting with a group of men he knew. Mum also saw this male cabal. She put on a very mean look to her face. Whatever they were plotting, she did not like it. They gave each other the thumbs up as if an agreement had been reached.

Dad came back to tell her he was going to the nearby pub for a swift half. Mum grumbled about being left on her own to look after Tom and myself. One of the other men's wife had a sharper tongue.

She told her husband, if more than one pint was drunk, he would be sleeping with the dog that night.

The men strutted off up the road.

I knew Mum had a grump on, so I decided to get out of clouting distance. I went to the coach behind. There was Eclipse bored with standing around. She wanted to be running and playing with me. Dusk was edging softly into night.

Eclipse's mum insisted neither of us must leave the confines of the coach park and we had to stay in shouting distance.

A few steps away I was Wild Bill Hickok and Eclipse became Annie Oakley. We were on the North American Plains, in the time of the Wild West. The coaches changed into buffalo. As we walked through the herd we shot them, because that is what cowboys did.

Parked amid these big beasts by comparison small, squatted a camper van. Eclipse said it was a baby bison. We did not shoot the infant. I fed it with grass.

Eclipse screamed. The noise blasted my ears. She pointed to a flaming light in the sky. It was a Dragon. I yelled in terror; even louder than her. We ran away as fast as our little legs would take us.

I found myself running down a dirt track. The coach park became a far distance. We ran and ran for what felt like forever.

Each time the two of us paused to catch our breath, we would look around to see the Dragon, still in gritty pursuit.

Hand in hand we ran. Trapped by our own terror. The track led into a great forest, black with the shadows of night. Eclipse said safety lay in hiding among the trees. That was not to be.

A huge giant blocked our way. Beside him stood an even larger monster than he. My heart thumped loud. Are we to be devoured by the dragon or eaten by the gruesome twosome in front.

The titan bellowed out why were we on his land? I pointed to the sky behind and told him a dragon wanted to eat us. He let out a gruff chuckle.

The colossus lifted me up. I screamed. Was he going to make me the first course of his dinner.

I got plonked on the back of the really huge monster. My legs could only straddle the broad beast by sitting next to his neck and clinging tight onto the mane.

Another loud scream. This time it did not come from my throat. Eclipse had been lifted up and put on the back of the monster. To stop herself falling off she had to cling onto me for dear life.

A sword came into my hand. The pair of us were told to face the fear we had run away from. I was to fight the dragon!

The monster lumbered forward and headed for the fiend we had ran from. The dragon saw me armed and shouting defiance. Did I see fear in that grotesque face. He used great magic to disappear in a puff of smoke. Eclipse and I cheered at his running away.

The monster cantered into the coach park. By him strode the mighty goliath. I was triumphant. I had saved the world from a fire breathing dragon.

The people waiting to get on the coaches were mute and seemed not to be bothered about it all. As this dragon slaying troupe came by Eclipse's coach, we paused. Her Dad hoisted her off our steed and carried her onto their awaiting lift home. I had no chance to say goodbye.

The giant was given a shilling by Eclipse's mum. I thought that was a bit rum. He should have been too old to get pocket money.

We moved on, minus Eclipse, to where my carriage awaited. The giant hoisted me off his monster and presented the hero of the hour to Mum. Every detail of that super adventure was imparted to her. She did not seem to listen, and ushered me onto the bus. The driver sat fidgety in his seat with the engine running. His eagerness to get home showed in every twitch of his face.

Mum put me in the seat next to Tom. I noted Dad's absence. A woman went off to round up the missing husbands.

A little later, the truants returned. That lady guided them onto the coach with the skill of a shepherd. They got booed by the other passengers for delaying the bus. Dad flopped himself down next to Mum. He was not her favourite person at that moment in time.

The charabanc Eclipse was on moved off. She waved me goodbye as the vehicle passed. It reached the road and stopped for a moment before turning left. Our coach followed, to the park exit, then veered to the right.

Still excited I told Tom of my epic adventure. My brother gave me a much more prosaic version of the same events. He had kept an eye on Eclipse and myself in the coach park.

He saw us stuffing clumps of grass into the exhaust pipe of a camper van. Then in the darkening sky Tom observed a comet. It held the name Arend-Roland. He knew all this because of watching that new Astronomy programme on the telly.

A feature of this solar body was it flew backwards in the sky. An action caused by the gravitational pull of the Sun. Also it had two tails that looked as if they were on fire.

Tom had laughed himself silly at the reaction of Eclipse and I when we spotted that strange light in the sky. He chuckled like mad when we ran screaming for our lives down that farm track.

A hundred yards down the path, a farm worker halted our flight and put us on the back of his plough horse. He gave me a stick to wave about. The comet then became hidden by clouds. Gently the old ploughman led his plodding Norfolk Punch into the coach park.

My brother always had a cold eye view of the world. When Tom grew up he was doomed to become an accountant.

Cricket Is A Strange Animal!

by Sean Langley

Sport has the capacity to paste indelible images into the scrapbook that is your memory! For me, none more so than this, barely credible but true, cricket story; a tale of the most joyous innings I have ever witnessed.

The Vultures Gathered

The new batsman strode to the wicket with what seemed a familiar languid gait, reminiscent of a Christian entering the Colosseum to face the lions. Only, they didn't play much cricket in Rome. Around him, opponents gathered like vultures, sensing further success. The batsman projected determination.

Assuming his stance at the crease he awaited the bowler, who was now positioned at the start of his run-up. Was I watching the great West-Indian, Clive Lloyd? Was I about to witness our own Andrew (Freddie) Flintoff, or even Ben Stokes, at their belligerent best?

Oh, no! This was the early 1980's, and I was umpiring a junior's match between my own club, Gosport Borough, and Droxford; played out on that village's remote recreation ground deep in the heart of rural Hampshire, on a warm damp summer's evening. You know the sultry kind we get in England?

The batsman? He was young Ian Collins, a big-hitting fifteen-year-old from the Rowner estate, in Gosport. A kid of few words, but very amiable. Even so, he was one that many lads of his age would have to think twice about before taking his last Rolo!

The Tiger Panted

Everyone now ready, the fresh-faced bowler set off,

arms and legs pumping; approaching the crease he aimed his delivery, and the right-handed Collins thumped it towards a long leg-side boundary. A fieldsman gave chase, as the batsmen charged from end-to-end. Youthful voices screamed-out instructions to the fieldsman, as a third run was comfortably completed. This crescendo of excitement only served to confuse; the ball was returned by the fieldsman but, nowhere near his team-mates. Evading them all, it shot out towards the boundary on the other side; no-one was covering.

Briefly, the fielding side stood, almost motionless, and looked at each other in bewilderment; meanwhile, the batsmen set off running again. By the time the fielders had galvanised themselves, another three runs were nearing completion. But…, hold-on! A run-out opportunity emerged. The ball was now on its way in from the cover boundary and Collins, panting like a tiger, flailed away in an effort to reach his crease safely.

Had Droxford learnt quickly? Not a bit of it! The ball had been returned by the fieldsman but, nowhere near his team-mates. Evading them all, it shot out towards the boundary on the other side; again! The batsmen, scarcely able to believe it or, for that matter, able to catch their breath, set off running yet again.

The Dog Barked
By now, noise levels had further escalated. The batting team yelled encouragement from the boundary, to their team-mates running themselves silly in the middle. Eleven fielders were still screaming at each other. Their coach was tearing his hair out in front of the small pavilion; and, some spectators (not that there were many) were rolling about laughing. All of which had awakened a small dog, who was sitting

over by the pitch roller and had now joined in, barking madly. An apt phrase in the circumstances!

This time, though, the fielders restored some sanity, and only two more runs were added before the ball was safely into the wicket-keeper's gloves. Even so, amidst the mayhem, Collins had managed to score an implausible eight runs from his very first ball.

The excitement calmed momentarily, and the bowler set off once more from the height of his run up. The adrenalin, not just his arms and legs, was pumping now as he reached the crease. Straining with effort, he emitted a groan. The bowler's aim was slightly out, but Collins' aim was true. Straining with effort, he too emitted a groan. The ball was clubbed cleanly, sailing over the long-on boundary for six runs. I raised my arms to signal to the scorers. It was a super shot. A proper cricket shot, if you like, not a slog.

The Frog Crouched

All the same, this was remarkable entertainment. Once again, I resumed my umpiring position behind the stumps at the bowler's end. The wicket-keeper crouched, frog-like, behind the stumps at the batsman's end. Fielders had assumed their positions. The spectators, the coach, and the dog, were all silent now in dazed anticipation. Collins, steely-eyed, was ready. You could almost hear his heart thumping; and the bowler, ball in hand, set off again.

It was impossible to predict what the outcome may be this time. The expectation was palpable. In the event, it was, sadly, a huge anti-climax. Collins attempted to repeat the feat of the previous ball. Not one to die wondering, he missed and the ball hit the wicket. The stumps were shattered. So, I think, were we all. Normality returned.

He had been bowled just third ball for fourteen

runs. Ian Collins had certainly not scored the most dashing century I had ever seen; nor had he batted with the most style I had ever seen; nor had he put his side into a winning position by any means. Yet this was, and still is, the most incredible, unforgettable, and joyful innings I have ever witnessed. In modern terms, Collins achieved a strike rate of 467*. Now, that takes some doing, however long the innings lasts; especially when you consider he failed to score off 33% of the deliveries he did face. Cricket is a strange animal at times!

* Note: Strike-rate indicates number of runs scored per 100 balls faced by the batsman.

Young Homer Changes the Songs of Troy

by Gwydion M. Williams

The old song-stitcher sat sleeping where he always sat, in the shade of a vast oak even older than he. Besides him were olives, oat cakes, goat's milk and wine. His wooden chair was the finest in the entire small Greek town: it had been carved long ago when he had arrived and amazed them. When he had sung superior versions of songs they had partly forgotten.

They now knew all of his songs. He had never made a new song, or changed an old one.

On a good day, he might still sing those beautiful and beloved songs. More often now he complained about young Homer, the apprentice who had run off more than two years ago. Or spoke of his dislike for other things no one else cared about. The Elders now wished he would die or go away, but said nothing. If one old man was openly disrespected, who knew where it would end?

The song-stitcher woke up. Briefly he seemed ready to sing something: perhaps a hymn to the setting sun. But then he frowned. Everyone knew with a sinking feeling that he would now complain rather than do his proper job.

"Young Homer wanted me to tell him of the Trojan War. I fought in a small raid against that ancient city, long after the war in which that brutal fool Achilles died of poison fish. He hears, but then weaves together stories from a dozen different times and places. Dumps them like scraps into stew to remake the famous Trojan Tragedy. Soon it is no longer Priam's story."

The man stopped and they hoped he'd go to

sleep again. Instead he went on:

"The Singing Sages left us the wonderful tale of Priam. How he went from ruin to great wealth and power, and then ruin again. A great king brought down by his pride towards his former friend, High King Agamemnon. That was three generations after Achilles: I gave him the full family history. He recalls it perfectly, but then sings otherwise. Makes his own songs on high matters, as if he were a new Singing Sage. Well, many young fools do so. I have seen five generations proudly devise songs that are now forgotten – yet they sung within the True Histories. All but young Homer, who sings lies."

The villagers listened, but did not care. What was truth in songs, indeed? Many queens secretly lay with lowly men, or with women or even with beasts. But to birth a creature with the head of a bull – ridiculous. Those who had seen real wars knew that Hercules could not have been as strong as they said. Nor met exotic monsters in lands that had no perils beyond lions and dull cruel bandits. Still, the old song-stitcher had once sung beautifully of Hercules, inspiring young men to boldness that their elders could then restrain. They owed him much for what he had once been: a vigorous middle-aged man with an astounding voice. A singer of half-forgotten legends.

Before the song-stitcher came, everyone knew that there had been twelve labours of Hercules, but remembered only seven. One of those must have been twisted by a passing prankster. The newly arrived singer – rhapsodist, he called himself, a word new to them – had pointed out that Hercules kissing each hydra-head before chopping it off was ridiculous. He had then sung them the true verses, how he had staunched the neck to stop two heads growing. Had sung splendid verses about the other eleven labours, and much else besides.

Now the man sung less, and brooded on his quarrel with young Homer. But he had been there when most of the Elders had been young warriors. When the men of middle age had been children. Who could doubt that he must be given wine and milk and oat-cakes, and olives when they were ripe? Also the largest and best portions of meat when an animal was slaughtered in honour of god or goddess. (Those powerful, jealous, and sometimes cruel powers were thankfully content with the smoke and essence, so mere humans could dare to eat the flesh and suck the bones.)

The song-stitcher looked around angrily, as if he thought Homer might have sneaked back. In his better days he had gone along with the regional custom of blind singers, which had not been known on the strange island of Crete where he had been born. That he had left for reasons unknown: perhaps a crime, perhaps a feud between powerful families. He had once been eager to please. He now assumed he could stay till he died and act just as he wished, which was sadly true. His blind-man's staff lay forgotten in the dust. He would sometimes wave it as he was supposed to. More often nowadays he would not bother.

The man began to hum something. People stopped and waited in the hope that he would sing. His voice was not what it had been, but was still far better than anyone else now that young Homer had left. But then his anger returned:

"The young fool twisted the story of King Paris Alexandros. Made him the son of King Priam rather than his great-grandfather. Perhaps he stole or lured the wife of a neighbouring King, though it could have been another Prince Paris. I told him there were several, just as the Egyptians had far too many Pharaohs called Ramesses after the great one. But he merged the tale with the famous abduction of Helen of Sparta. I told him: everyone knows that it was King Theseus who stole Helen and held her until he died. Perhaps of exhaustion from his pretty captive, but his legend will never be forgotten. It has been growing with the years, indeed, with the bull-masked High Priest of Crete transformed into a half-human monster whose killing becomes heroic, rather than the casual butchery it actually was. Still, young Homer cannot write out Theseus and expect to be believed. Or would he have it that Helen was abducted twice? As likely that she hatched from an egg!

"King Achilles slew King Alexandros in honest battle, but then dragged his body behind his chariot and let it rot unburnt and unburied, which was shameful. And then died of poison fish, most likely an accident. Young Homer has invented a vengeful princess. Captive princesses don't do the cooking. The horrible Achilles had plenty of enemies, and perhaps no friends.

"But he now wants to give him one. Patroclus slayer of Clysonymus, who lived much later. He gives King Priam extra sons and daughters, as if six of each were not right and proper and according to the cycle of the months. And he was adding better tales for that savage trickster Odysseus. He's a perfectly good villain, quarrelling with and finally destroying the thug Great Ajax. Why make him a hero?"

The man spat and added: "everyone knows that Odysseus drowned with all but one of his men on his way home. Perished due to the anger of the gods. That his son was murdered when his father was reported dead, or else was killed when he tried to throw out his mother's suitors. There are also stories of two or three fellows turning up claiming to be the lost King of Ithaca. All failed. Yet young Homer says, the audience likes Odysseus. He gives him the tales of Ulixes and other lost sea-farers. He makes Odysseus a hero rather than a sinner."

He then went silent and slept some more. Everyone hoped he'd forget the misdeeds of Homer when he woke up. He did indeed to that – but only to begin another rant:

"These are degenerate days. Most men cannot read, or use the worthless squiggles of the Phoenicians. I am almost the last who knows the word-wisdom of the Elder Peoples of my beloved Crete. Their strange language I never learned well: all wisdom is everywhere fading. But wise men took their signs and made them fit for Greek. Once the wise High Kings of Mycenae made sure it was used. But Mycenae is gone; her Lion Gate a ruin. All now forgotten except for Agamemnon, and him just for the pointless wars he fought."

The old man sighed. "I looked once at the Phoenician system. It has far too few signs to show civilised speech: no more than a couple of dozen. I myself know all 193 signs of the Cretan system, but who nowadays will take the time to learn them? Young Homer would not. He says that he hears the words well enough, and replays the sounds in his head. That script would only confuse him."

The old man sighed again. "These Phoenicians choose the leaders of their cities by voting, as if a city were no more than a war-band where allied kings must debate and decide. Well, that will never get a grip on Greece. We still know that cities must choose kings from the famous families that have at least a little of the blood of the gods."

The small town acknowledged a king in a nearby city, but governed itself by Elders. It had never actually had voting and did not want it. Elders chose new Elders, and everyone talked until everyone was agreed, or at worst was tired of arguing against the majority. None of them claimed even a little of the blood of the famous gods, though one man's grandmother claimed to have been raped by a satyr. Most people knew it was to explain a baby she'd had by an unknown man, but her family had been too powerful for it to be openly called a lie.

Regarding writing, they knew that if you learned the peculiar Phoenician markings, you could set down speech and let a stranger look at it to summon up the same words. But only two men knew the markings, useful for trade. No one had any use for it in common matters. Some priests said that using it for Divine Verse would be a blasphemy: that was a matter for priests and song-stitchers, who had vast memories for rituals and songs. But the townspeople had gradually realised that their song-stitcher had a memory that might not be so perfect. That he had several odd objects that he called scrolls, marked with the strange and ancient Cretan symbols. There, perhaps, were stored at least some of the songs he sung. It might be a blasphemy, but they had seen no ill-luck. Or none except for him quarrelling with young Homer.

Having lapsed into silence for a while, the old man grabbed his stick, got up and waved the stick at the sun, which was now almost set. "By the Mother and by her younger brother and husband the Thunderer, I call down and invoke..." The man trailed off, looking confused. "I call down and invoke..." he repeated, but then fell forward flat on his face. Several people rushed to help him. The best of the town's three doctors attended him. But said that he knew not the sickness, unless it was old age. And soon pronounced him dead.

"Well, do we burn or bury him?" asked one Elder. "Did he tell us how they do it in Crete?"

"Never did say much about his life there" replied another. "Let's burn him, on a very high pyre and with the sacrifice of whatever animals we can spare. He was a great man once, which I find more real than his sad final decline. Burn his body."

"Burn his scrolls with him, just in case the gods are offended by them" said a third. There were nods of agreement. Then the Elder who had spoken first said "and do we now try to get another song-stitcher? Or just wait till one turns up?"

"Is there one who'd come to our small town?"

"Assuredly. Young Homer, who we know already. I liked him and have asked after him. A merchant told me he is in the citadel of a small king some way away. But might be glad to leave, because a powerful priest there does not like the way he is changing the Tragedy of Troy. Is offended by the extra deeds given to gods and goddesses, not all of them flattering."

"Could be dangerous for young Homer. If they have a bad year, the priest might blame him and convince the king of it. So would he come?"

"We can ask. He may want to change more than he dare do there. The merchant likes songs, and didn't care if they were true or not. Can't sing better than a frog, but he makes up words very nicely. Between them, they have changed a lot more than our poor old song-stitcher was offended by. They've cooked up a much better ending for Troy than the one we know. I always felt it spoiled the tale, having the Greeks wait ten months and then swarm in and kill all after an earthquake cracked the walls. If it was Poseidon's wrath against Troy, why didn't he do it earlier?

"But there is another story from a different city that the merchant wants to use instead. An army besieged a strong city and then went away, but left behind a large wooden horse as an offering to Poseidon. The men of the city came out, took a look and thought it best to burn it, since it might carry a curse. Give Poseidon something else and something of greater value, so he'd not be angry. So they began gathering wood and pouring oil, but then the top of the horse opened and a frightened little fellow popped out."

"A miracle? A man born of horse?"

"No, a fool who had hoped the horse would be taken into the city. That he could then come out at night and open the gate for the army, who were lurking nearby just in case. That he could wave a torch to signal them."

"He thought that the men of the city would have built a wall, but not keep a watch on the gate at night?"

"Of course there was a guard. Maybe he thought he could overpower them, though I doubt it would work with even half-decent guards. It was foolish, and the men of the city fell about laughing. Pardoned the man who had tried to get them all killed, though of course he was made a slave. But well treated, because they see him as clown."

They all laughed at that. But then one said "But Troy did fall. Will young Homer have the wise King Priam fall for such a simple trick?"

"He has some coils of story still to devise. I think he plans to make the horse bigger: too big to bring in without breaking a gate."

"Taking it even further from the true tale."

"Does that matter? If it entertains, if it teaches the young to do the right thing, need it be true? Are the songs we know always true?"

There were nods of agreement. But then the oldest Elder said "We must also stop calling him 'young Homer'. We tell him to make himself look older. That he must act seriously when seen by the common people. He can jest with we Elders as much as he likes, but not in public. And he must act as if he were born blind. Or has gone blind since he last lived here."

"Why? Only the children believed the old fellow was really blind."

"Yes, but the young and the women think it proper. They believe that gods and spirits watch their every action, and so live better lives and lie less than they otherwise would. We Elders know that the gods are mostly busy and neglectful, and can be bribed to overlook almost anything. But we have the most to lose. We must not confuse them."

"True. Yes, let young Homer – let the distinguished rhapsodist Homer play with words as he pleases. His work might even become famous beyond this little town of ours"

And so it was. The little town was later destroyed and forgotten. But the words of 'young Homer' were to last beyond all measure.

Background

Troy was a real place, but the standard picture from archaeology does not fit Homer:

Troy was a very old settlement, and not Greek. Perhaps became a western extension of the Hittite Empire. Or an unknown people with a loose allegiance to them.

Troy also traded with the Mycenaean Greeks, whose High Kings sometimes had Great King status. One Trojan king had the part-Greek name Priam Alexandros, suggesting intermarriage. Maybe a mix of trade and war with the many rival Greek cities.

Troy VI was as rich and powerful as Homer shows: the city's high point. It existed in the right era, but was destroyed by an earthquake, not warfare.

Troy VIIa was a shadow of Troy VI. It was

eventually sacked and burnt, perhaps by the enigmatic Sea People. Many Greek cities were also destroyed in this period.   Some, including Agamemnon's Mycenae, were never rebuilt.

Troy became an unimportant Greek city. But they remembered it as the setting of Homer's epic.

If this is right – there are many disputes – then my imagined Tragedy of Troy was also not the historic truth.   If Priam existed, he ruled the weak and impoverished Troy VIIa.

Interestingly, Greek legend has general ruin for the Greeks after the fall of Troy. Perhaps a hazy memory of the fall of Late Bronze Age civilisation.

As for writing: early Greeks wrote in Linear B, adapted from the older and undeciphered Linear A. Later Greeks got the alphabet and probably the idea of republican government from the Phoenicians.

See   https://gwydionmadawc.com/050-about-science-fiction/priams-tragedy-and-the-wrath-of-achilles/ for more on the history behind this fiction.

One woman's trash is another man's treasure

by Hilary Hopker

When you sit in exactly the same spot in London for eighteen hours you see a lot of things. Against a backdrop of tourists, taxis and pigeons, I have seen a young man in a top hat and a monocle, a dwarf carrying a poodle in a handbag and three women all doing the walk of shame in exactly the same sequined dress. The one thing I have not seen however is the one thing I was sent to look for - Sue Perkins.

I decide to call Eddie. No one ever wants to call their editor and admit failure, so first I puff on the last of my e-cigarette, and the damn thing needs charging, and then search for "Bulldog" in my contacts.

Three rings before I have the delight of Eddie booming in my ear, "Jack, you had better be phoning in your copy, it's close to deadline and I'm a splash short of a newspaper here!"

"Eddie mate, she ain't here I tell you. I've been here all night, no lights, no noises, the queen of cakes has left the building!"

"I'm not your mate, Jack. I'm the editor. You phone here in the next hour with an exclusive on the nation's Bake Off babe or the next paper you get a byline on is your P45," and with that he hangs up.

I turn to the snapper and sigh, "We've got to come up with an exclusive in an hour, or next time I'm sent out onto the street to do a job, it's as a busker."

"Shit, I miss the Diana days," she says, "back of a bike, stalking your prey with long lenses, get 'em in your sights and bang, bang, there's your front page, easy. All this respecting their privacy, waiting for them to walk out of their house and give you a smile, it's giving the paparazzi a bad name. Now I'm competing with every camera phone in the world. Last week I was scooped by two kids with an iPhone who got photo bombed by a gorilla. A gorilla for Christ's sake."

My snapper's not just my snapper; she's my girlfriend too, which is lucky because journalism's a lonely world. Hacks are notoriously hard to live with. They are never in and they only go on holiday if it's a press trip. Half of them get shot covering war zones, the other half are drunks and all of them are seriously addicted to twitter. In this game you kiss goodbye to family life, sobriety and your washing machine.

The only people who understand hacks are other hacks and snappers. Snappers are journalism's socially retarded side. They don't do interviews and sweet-talking; they snap away and shout "over here darling, one more for the camera!" A super cynical bunch, the only thing I've ever seen a snapper get emotional over was a royal baby.

I couldn't believe my luck when I was sent on a job six months ago and found out the snapper was a girl. Karen understood me instantly and there's no one else I'd rather be crouching outside a celebrity's house with, for half a day and a night.

I look at her, her beautiful long brown hair tied back with an elastic band, bright blue eyes a contrast to her pale, slightly yellowing skin. Her slim figure in tight black jeans and a snug leather jacket. She's biting her lip and if I hadn't last seen my toothbrush two days ago, I could kiss her right now.

"So we old school it," she says, shrugging. Locking her eyes onto mine she declares, "It's time for Top Cat."

I groan, "Oh no, not Top Cat. I didn't bring any gloves."

"Darling no one ever does. Top Cat works, it's

just messy."

"Ok," I reluctantly agree. "Let's do it!" and we head for the bins.

Top Cat's an affectionate term for emptying out a celebrity bin to find a story. You never know what those celebs throw away. Find a supermodel with a bin full of choc wrappers - then she's a secret bulimic. A game show host with a bin full of porn mags and cotton knickers? He's a paedophile. Easy headlines, but its dirty work.

So what's in Sue Perkin's bin? We empty it carefully across the concrete at the back of her house and spread it out. Banana skins, carrot peel, yoghurt pots and a half finished packet of granola.

"She's eaten two packets of ginger cake and a box of French Fancies," declares Karen.

"Gold for a supermodel or a daytime TV presenter," I say, "but she's the queen of cakes, so no one will be surprised she's acquainted with Mr. Kipling."

"Bank statement!" cries Karen, peeling a tea bag off a damp piece of paper and handing it over.

"So is she loaded or secretly broke?" I ask, as I scan the statement. "Phone contract, petrol, shops at Waitrose, eyebrow wax, Topshop jumper and train tickets... damn, no balance, it's torn off the bottom."

"Nothing there then," says Karen.

We root around the rest, a half-eaten Naan bread, an empty bottle of chardonnay, two kit kat wrappers, cotton buds, organic veg wrappers, empty pot of jam and a broken light bulb.

"A burnt oven mit would have been good," muses Karen, holding up an old tea towel she's just found.

"Queen of cakes burns down millionaire mansion with bad bun batch," I retort and smile.

I look at my watch, "P45 minus forty," I say

sadly.

"So we fake it," decides Karen, wiping tomato juice covered fingers down her jeans.

"All right. So, what's the best secret you could find in Sue Perkin's bin?" I ask.

"Let's think. Lesbian BBC TV presenter, national treasure, queen of cake, witty, musical, not concerned about her figure, got a girlfriend, no kids."

"A dead kitten?"

"Cat in the bin has been done. Besides, you can't fake a dead kitten without finding a dead kitten for me to snap."

"Secret boyfriend?"

"Possibly. We need a box of aftershave and two condoms for that."

"A ripped baby grow?" I suggest.

"No kids remember. She's a lesbian."

"They all adopt though, don't they? African orphans usually."

"So we need a brochure for an orphanage, a receipt for a flight to Kenya and a Mothercare catalogue," states Karen in practical tones.

I look at my watch. "No time to find an orphanage brochure and a flight receipt, might just manage a Mothercare catalogue."

"Got it!" declares Karen, "back in a mo!" and with that she roars off on her bike.

Ten minutes later, as I'm sweating my career out of my unwashed armpits, Karen reappears with a small chemist's bag.

"Pregnancy test kit!" she declares, "secret boyfriend or longed for IVF baby!"

"Brilliant!" I exclaim, "go snap it and I'll call the copy in."

Karen crouches down behind the bins then reappears to arrange the rubbish so it looks like we found the kit in the trash, right next to the French

Fancies.

I jabber down the phone to Eddie, "The queen of cakes has a secret - everyone thought that the only tummy bulge she would ever have is a cake baby, but secret sources reveal she's desperate for a child of her own. Friends say she's been to an IVF clinic and is rumoured to want a baby so badly she is now looking for a boyfriend!"

Eddie laps it up and passes it on to the subs for a headline.

"Good work, Jack!" He declares and with that my career is saved and I go home to shower and sleep.

Karen wakes me with the paper in her hand, "Look!" she demands.

My bleary eyes take a few moments to focus. I read the headline, "Pregnant Perkins?" and smile. I don't need to read the story, as I already know what it says.

"Great!" I mumble and turn over, willing myself back to sleep.

Karen shakes me, "No look!" she demands, sounding serious.

I pick the paper up and stare at it again. Everything seems fine, my by-line on the story, a library photo of Perkins and some shots of the rubbish Karen took.

"What is it?" I ask her, baffled.

"Look at the photo," Karen says, sounding irritated now.

"Which one?" I ask her, "Perkins or the rubbish?"

"The one I took, Dumbo!" she says.

I stare at the photo, there's the pregnancy test stick thing next to the French Fancies box and a banana skin.

"Yeah it's great," I say, wondering if she thinks

I'm not taking her work seriously enough.

Karen sighs.

I admit defeat. "Ok what's the matter?" I ask her. "Am I missing something?"

Karen points to the photo and talks to me like I'm a three year old, "see that stick there?"

"Yeah..." I answer.

"Well that's a pregnancy test kit."

"Yeah..." I agree.

"And how many pink lines do you see on it?"

I stare at the photo, "Two," I reply, hoping this is the answer she's looking for.

"Well done!" she says patronisingly. "Do you know what that means?" she asks.

"No, not really," I admit.

"Well just before we took the pic, I realised the test kit would only look any good if it was used, so I went behind the bins and err... used it. It takes a few minutes for those things to work and we were in such a rush I just arranged the rubbish and snapped. I never paid any attention to it until now."

I feel like there's a big penny inside my head that should be dropping, but it's getting stuck.

"Two lines means you're pregnant," she says.

The penny crashes. I leap up and hug her. "Hey that's amazing!" I say, tears pricking at my eyes.

"It's a bit of a shock," says Karen.

"Yeah, for me too," I agree, "but in a good way," I say smiling.

I'm making tea for us both when Karen walks into the kitchen brandishing her phone. "What have you done?" she exclaims. "You've got a thousand re-tweets already!"

"Sorry." I say, looking down at my feet, "Couldn't resist."

She looks at her screen and reads aloud, "I

made Sue Perkins pregnant! #Whoknew"

I shrug my shoulders and smile.

Karen picks up the paper of the kitchen table, rolls it into a tube and smacks me hard across the head.

"Bloody twitter!"

"Bloody hacks!"

"Actually I'm going to re-tweet that too!" she says with a grin.

Weird Pete

by Emilie Lauren Jones

"I mean, he's not horrible - just weird. Not like creepy weird but like train-spotting, stamp-collecting weird. I don't think he's ever smiled...Just don't take too much notice."

Pete re-tidied pieces of paper, moved the calculator twice then cleared his throat, but his ears were still subjected to Jane's overly-loud whispers from the desk opposite.

Jane motioned the lady she was saying this to towards his desk. Pete watched as her wavy mass of dark blonde hair, like caramel spilling out of a chocolate bar came closer to him. He flushed with the realisation that he had been staring at the newcomer and he felt cross with himself – now he had just proved that he was weird.

"And this is the lovely Pete!" Jane said then laughed.

Jane's laugh was reminiscent of an overly-excited seal and it made Pete want to cover his ears, instead he made do with digging his fingernails into his palms. He tried to smile but he had never been able to - he was not sure how other people did it. He sent the instruction to his mouth but it merely lifted his lips and showed his teeth.

"...And this is our new arrival, Beth," Jane finished.

Beth's smile shone out between the freckles on her face.

"Hi!" Beth said.

Pete nodded and thought that he should say something back but before he had the chance, Jane was guiding Beth away, no doubt pleased that she could tick 'introduce Weird Pete' off her list.

"So, welcome to the Payroll Department! I'll come with you to your desk and we can get you logged on to the computer..." Jane said to her.

Pete watched as Beth was directed further away from him. He brushed his hand through his hair, attempting to recover from having the most beautiful lady he had ever seen standing at his desk. Not that it mattered; Beth would just be another person who took no notice of him – people didn't take notice of you if you were weird.

Pete began making his daily to-do list:
-	Check and reply to emails – 9:20
-	Register new starters – 10:00

He paused. Beth swished across the office. Where was she going? Ah - to the stationary cupboard. The desire to follow her rushed through him but he couldn't go and stand in the cupboard with her; that would just confirm that he was weird. Before going back to his list, he glanced at the computer clock: 9:09 already? How had that happened? He always had the list written by 9:05. Pete felt his stomach knot up and his face flush. His routine was ruined, now he would be behind all day. Should he change the times he had written or try and work faster? 9:12. Three minutes left to finish the list and answer the emails. He tapped his pen.

"Pete?"

He looked straight up into the glowing face of Beth.

"I'm really sorry to disturb you but I can't find the staples. Would you mind helping me?"

Pete rubbed his forehead. Three minutes to help Beth, finish the list and answer emails. He blinked.

"If you're busy I can ask someone else."

Yes he was busy but he wanted to be the one to find the staples for her. Out of everyone in the office she had chosen to ask him; not Barry who went to the gym every night and not Yasu who knew the lyrics to every song in the top 40. Beth had picked him. He stood up quickly – he would find the staples.

"Thanks," Beth said, following him to the cupboard.

"Left side, shelf two, seventh box."

Pete nodded. Should he wait with her while she picked out the ones she wanted or leave her to it? Before he could make up his mind, Beth had finished and was waiting for him to move out of the way.

"Right," he said, moving aside.

"Thanks, Pete. Hopefully I won't need to bother you again."

He blinked. He wanted her to bother him again.

"If you need anything else though..."

She smiled and squeezed his shoulder. His stomach fluttered under the touch of her sleek, tanned hand before returning to their separate desks.

By lunchtime, Pete still hadn't caught up so decided that he would quickly walk to the shop and have his lunch at his desk. Taking his usual route past the red bench and across the edge of the park, he ran his fingers through his too-long hair and felt pleased that tomorrow he had booked the morning off to have it trimmed. He wondered if Beth would notice?

'You look so smart, Pete,' he imagined her saying.

Would that be the sort of thing Beth would say? He was debating this when a bike zoomed past sending a cascade of muddy water across his white shirt. A low growling noise echoed around his throat. He hated bikes: he had always hated bikes. It had been a day just like today when his father had tried to teach him to ride without stabilisers. Even now he recalled the rolling of his father's eyes and the firmness of his father's hands dragging him back towards that monster – it's spinning pedals mocking him...

Pete walked faster and faster, closing his jacket around him to cover up the stains but it was no good; he knew they were there. At the counter, the cashier stared at him – maybe she could sense the mud covered top he was hiding? He pulled at his clothes all the way back to the office.

He strode through the reception area with his head down then turned his chair to face the wall whilst he ate.

"Pete?"

It was Beth. Mouth filled with food he decided that the best response was a backward wave.

"Sorry, you're busy – I'll come back."

He blinked realising that he had given her the wrong response.

"Wait!" he said but it came out more like: "muait!" due to his full mouth.

At the same time he span his chair around to face her and his jacket flew open revealing a mass of stained shirt. There was no time to pull his jacket shut – she had seen. He rested the remainder of his sandwich on top of its packaging.

"Oh no! What happened?"

"Rushing and there was a bike and a puddle and..."

She started to laugh; if Jane's laugh was a tornado then Beth's was a summer's breeze.

"Poor you! I bet you can't wait to get home and change."

His face began to cool returned to a normal temperature.

"No. I hate mud and dirt."

"I hate wet socks," she said, "you know when you don't realise your shoe has a hole in it and then it rains!"

"Yes, that's horrible too."

"I was just coming to ask about tomorrow, you know, the charity event. Is there a theme? I don't want to come in wearing the wrong thing on my second day!" she said.

"Umm... yes, the theme is purple, it's..."

He was interrupted by an intrusive, seal-like screech: Jane.

"Don't be asking him! He never bothers with dressing up, do you? Miserable sod!"

More screeching laughter vibrated the air around him. His fingers twitched.

"I always pay my money," was the best response he could think of.

"I never said you didn't but I've already seen you've booked the morning off tomorrow," Jane said.

She turned her attention back to Beth.

"It's purple – so purple top or a bit of face-paint if you're feeling brave!"

Jane put her arm around Beth's shoulder and guided her away.

"If you have any questions come and find me – he's best left alone – doesn't do fun."

Jane probably thought that she was whispering. Pete rubbed his hair; at least Jane had gone and he had said that he always paid his money so Beth wouldn't think he was a selfish weirdo – just a weirdo who didn't dress up. He didn't see Beth again for the rest of the day and at exactly 17:00 he switched off the computer, picked up his bag and left. He couldn't wait to get home, the first thing he would do was to put a wash on.

As Pete sat in the hairdresser's chair the next morning, he felt comfortable in the knowledge that the charity day festivities were going on without him and that by lunchtime, when he returned, the face-paint would be smudged and any fancy dress outfits half-removed. It would almost be a normal day.

Pete was invited to move to the sink area; he felt hands massaging his scalp but they were smaller, skinnier... He jolted forwards and span around, towel flying into the sink.

"Is everything okay, Sir?" the young lad asked.

"You're not Laura," replied Pete.

"No, I'm here on work experience; it's my job to wash the hair then Laura will cut it.

"Well I'm not sure I..."

"Is everything okay?" asked another hairdresser.

"I was just saying that I'm washing the hair this week, Miss," the boy replied.

People were starting to look over.

"Is there a problem?" the other hairdresser repeated.

"No," Pete said.

The hairdresser rolled her eyes and Pete knew that they thought he was weird. He didn't like these strange hands touching him and he hated the invasive smell of the strange shampoo the lad was using. Why did he need to use new shampoo; why couldn't he use the one that Laura always used? Pete squeezed his nails into his skin until the ordeal was over.

At last Laura took over and he was sat in his usual chair. Pete started to relax as she snipped his hair. But something wasn't right; maybe it was the strange smelling shampoo? Laura stopped mid-sentence and he tried to read her expression.

He watched her reflection talking to the young lad who pointed to a dark mixture. Laura shook her head. Blood rushed around his body and he pulled at one side of his hair. That's what was wrong – as his previously straw-coloured hair was drying, it was turning a definite shade of purple!

His feet tapped.

"Pete, I'm so sorry..." Laura began.

"Turn it back!" he shouted.

"It would make it worse – you can't put dye on top of dye. I'm really sorry."

"What am I going to do?"

"It's not permanent so we can either wait for it to fade over the next few days or shave it all off."

"What!"

"I really am sorry, I'll finish the cut, I won't charge for it, of course, and then I'll do it for free next time too. It washes out in ten washes, I promise."

Pete stared back at his reflection. How could he go to work like this? What would they say? What would Beth think?

"Why have you done this to me?" he shouted and no longer caring if the whole salon had turned to see who the weird person causing a scene was, he grabbed his things and rushed out – his hair still damp and ruffled.

An hour later Pete shuffled passed the reception area, placed his money in the charity box and headed straight to his desk. He had never had time off work.

He pulled his collar close and logged in to his computer.

"Oh my God!"

He heard seal noises and clapping before he saw her – Jane.

"No way! Everyone, Pete has only gone and dyed his hair purple for the charity day! Well, I never saw that coming!"

She screeched away; purple deely-boppers bobbing manically above her head.

He sank further into his chair and ruffled his hand though his disastrous hair. Someone squeezed his shoulder – Beth.

"When did you decide to do that?"

She smiled, nodding to his hair.

"I didn't decide," he said.

"What do you mean?" she paused, "please this isn't because of what Jane said yesterday?"

"No! It was a mistake. The stupid hair washer used the wrong bottle."

"Oh gosh, Pete! Are you okay?"

"I look like a weirdo."

"No you don't – you look fantastic! Is it permanent?"

"No. It comes out in ten washes."

"That's good," she sighed, "well not good, but it could be worse. What a great day for it to happen!"

Beth gestured at her own purple top and smiled as Yasu appeared over her shoulder.

"No way! It is true!" Yasu said.

Pete blinked. Yasu only ever spoke to him to say 'morning!' and 'night!' She must be there to laugh at him.

"That is so cool! I've always fancied purple hair – are you going to keep it like that?"

"No," Pete answered.

"He's just done it for today – for the charity event," Beth interrupted.

"That's really awesome, Pete. I never knew you were so passionate about the Guinea Pig sanctuary," Yasu said.

'I'm not,' he was going to reply but decided against it.

"Can I take a photo?"

Yasu swiped at her phone.

"Uh…"

"Nice hair, Pete!" said Barry, nodding on his way to the photocopier.

FLASH!

"Cheers! Catch you in a bit!" Yasu said, moving

back, face still fixed on her phone she narrowly avoided crashing into Jane.

"No phones!" Jane screeched, "and what is going on, why is Pete so popular all of a sudden? Back to your desks everyone, I'm sure we'd all like to go home on time tonight."

"I think someone's a bit jealous," Beth whispered.

Pete managed to work relatively undisturbed for the rest of the afternoon – he wasn't sure when it had happened but he no longer felt the need to pull his collar up. People smiled at him if they passed and once Yasu ran over to inform him that #PurplePete had 'got over a hundred likes on Insta,' which was already twelve more than when she'd had her nose ring 'done'.

The only real interruption was Jane, who, without warning came and sat at his desk. He stared at her trying to work out what was going on.

"As much as we all appreciate your little hair stunt, I feel that it is important to inform you that it must be gone by tomorrow."

Pete nodded.

"Well?"

He was unsure what she wanted him to do next.

"The purple will be gone tomorrow, won't it?" she persisted.

"Uh...It comes out in ten washes."

"Well I suggest that you give it a good ten washes tonight," she said.

Huffing, she clattered away with the chair.

"And don't think I didn't notice your muddy shirt yesterday," she called back.

He looked around to see if anyone had seen but the nearest person was Beth and she was tapping away on her computer keyboard. Crunching his fists, he turned his chair to the wall. Did Jane think that he liked the odd feel and smell of this ridiculous colour stuck to his own hair? Maybe yesterday he should have gone home and changed, but he would never have caught up. If only that stupid bike hadn't...

An email popped on to his screen – it was from Beth.

I told you she's jealous you've got all the attention! Don't worry about it – Yasu said you've inspired her to do hers purple tonight too! :-)

Pete turned towards Beth who put a finger to her lips, which he knew meant that he shouldn't say anything. He liked that Beth trusted him and suddenly he didn't care what Jane thought.

At 5pm exactly he switched his computer off, grabbed his jacket and bag and made his way out.

"Pete! Wait a second!" Beth called.

She was stuffing her things into her backpack whilst struggling to get her other arm into the sleeve of her jacket.

If he waited, he might be late home but he had to wait because Beth wanted him to.

"Sorry!" she said, arriving next to him; "Are you feeling okay after today's excitement?"

"Yes, actually, I've enjoyed it."

"I wanted to invite you to this thing I go to on a Saturday, a group of us cycle round the park; nothing too energetic, just a gentle ride around. Do you fancy coming along?"

He rubbed his face.

"Don't worry about it, I just thought I'd ask," she said.

"No, I'd like to see you on Saturday. It's just..."

"What is it?"

"I can't... uh... I can't, ride a bike," his face flushed as he said it.

"Oh, is that it?"

He nodded.

"Well we've got a tandem at the club too so you could hop on the back of there, one of the guys can go at the front for you, or I can?"

He nodded. She didn't seem to think it was weird.

"Saturday, what time does..."

"...That sounds good – I've always fancied a bit of bike riding..." Jane interjected.

"Oh, I don't think it would be your thing," Beth said and smiled sweetly.

"Nearly Two hundred likes!" Yasu said bouncing over to join them.

"Up to anything rock n' roll tonight, Pete?" Barry asked, flinging his gym bag over his shoulder.

"Just washing my hair."

He wasn't sure what was so funny but his ears enjoyed the tinkling of their laughter.

The Muse At Ten

by David Court

"You're late," said the Writer, leaning back in his chair and taking another sip of inadequately chilled Sauvignon Blanc. A cigarette was burning away in a crowded ashtray.

"I find that incredibly unlikely," said the Muse, "given that I'm a fictional construct solely set up for the purpose of this story. And anyway, I thought you'd given up smoking?"

"I had – or rather, I have," said the Writer as he sat back up and smoked the last of the cigarette. "Haven't smoked since December 2011, but I've come to the conclusion that I must still miss them on some fundamental level because a lot of my characters have the habit. And they can't do me any harm here, after all. But you already know all that, don't you?"

"Don't blame me for your character's smoking habit," tutted the Muse. "They're just peripheral details – and probably ones you throw in just to keep them busy between conversations. Long, tedious conversations. I'm responsible for the big stuff, not the minutiae that adds a bit of colour. I can't be doing it all myself, after all. I still need you. Although I'll be honest I'm not keen on this paragraph – tutted can't be a real word, surely? And it feels overlong, as though I've been wittering on for longer than the reader will be comfortable with."

"It sounds right," said the Writer defiantly, "so it's stopping in."

"There you go again."

"What?"

"There you go again. You have a real problem with any sort of criticism."

"I do not!"

"You're proving my point just by getting angry. Anyway, I digress – and that's really your job, isn't it? What did you want, anyway?"

"I just needed to clarify some details about our little – arrangement."

"What sort of details?" asked the Muse as he picked up the half-full bottle of wine on the table and began studying its label intently.

"I'm still not sure how it works. Sometimes you don't appear for days on end and sometimes you just give me too much stuff to handle. Could you not balance it all a bit? Spread it out?"

The Writer leaned over and grabbed the bottle back from the Muse and slammed it down on the table. The Muse, rather than appearing startled, simply sighed and rubbed his eyes for a few moments before placing his head in his hands.

Pinter himself would have been proud of the uncomfortable and lengthy silence that followed. Eventually, reluctantly, the Muse looked back up at the Writer.

"It doesn't work like that. It's never worked like that. I'm not just some production line of ideas, you know. I'm the bit of you that gets inspired by something you read or hear, or the bit that gets prompted by some mad dream you have at two in the morning"

"I realise that, but you can sometimes take ages. And then sometimes you give me ideas that have either been done before or just aren't very good."

"Hang on one minute, that's-"

"Where do I start - A blood bank that's run by Vampire or a story where the lead character has been dead all along? Cheers, mate - we've all seen The Sixth Sense, thanks. And the great one where the doctor invents technology that lets him swap brains with one of his patients so he can feel their pain without them needing to describe where they're hurting. Four bloody pages of that I wrote before I realised it wasn't going anywhere."

"But I-"

"And that's when you're not giving me ideas that I read somewhere else in a short story years back. There have even been times when I've found I've been ripping off my own work. In all honesty I'm not sure why I need you at all."

The Muse leaned back in his chair and blinked at the Writer.

"Is it my turn to talk now?" the Muse snapped, sarcastically.

"I'll take your silence as approval then," the Muse continued. "I think you sometimes forget how this all works. Those stories you're telling me about – that's not me, that's you. Without me those are all you'd get. When you get the good ones, the ones you're excited to show other people, the ones that don't remind you of anything else and writing them is a genuine pleasure -"

There was a few seconds silence before the Muse stood up and stretched his arms out wide and raised his voice.

"- those ones are my ones. But I can't do it alone."

The Writer looked sheepishly at his shoes for a few moments before he stood up and opened his arms wide. The Muse, calmer now, stood up. The two hugged.

"I get it now. Let's never fight again, Muse. One little last thing though."

"I'm listening?"

"I sometimes really struggle with endings."

The Muse laughed out loud, and the Writer could do nothing but watch as brilliant bright flowers in a myriad of hues erupted from the Muse's skin until he exploded in a beautiful cloud of fragrant white blossom.

The Writer drank the last of the glass of wine and raised the empty vessel into the air.

"Here's to you, Muse. I didn't expect that."

Body Language

by Ann Evans

With a contented sigh, Carol closed the book and set it aside, delighted with her newly gained knowledge.

Body Language – How to read others like a book.

Now she understood those mannerisms she'd always mistaken for irritating little habits they took on a fascinating new meaning. She couldn't wait to try it out.

The tube station next morning on her way to work was her first opportunity. She glanced at a man in a grey suit. Ultra smart, outwardly looking calm and relaxed, but Carol spotted the slight drumming of his fingers against his thigh and the rhythmic tapping of his foot.

Inwardly he was anxious, keen to get on with his busy day. Probably he had some meeting to attend, or an interview for a new job. Something important anyway. Moments later, when he glanced at his watch and his eyes fluttered briefly shut, Carol knew her assumption was spot on.

Next to come under her scrutiny was the youth in denims standing behind a pretty teenager. He was just a fraction too close to be as disinterested at he was trying to appear. And when the train finally came he took a seat right next to her. Carol sat opposite, observing.

Poor boy! she thought. The girl wasn't the slightest bit interested otherwise her crossed legs would have been crossed towards him – not away.

Carol felt elated, it was almost as if she could read people's minds.

Her day was more fun than usual, although her boss did ask if she was alright, saying that she was quieter than normal.

She was quiet because she was busy analysing the body language of her colleagues – not that she had any intention of telling them what she'd discovered about each of them. Like Jason actually being dependant on Lauren, and Penny envious of Jane's recent engagement.

When her husband Tony arrived home that evening and gave her the customary hug, Carol glowed happily. She'd often thought his usual greeting was done out of habit rather than anything else. But this time she looked up into his eyes and saw his pupils dilate – a sure sign that he was pleased to see her.

Dinner was unusually quiet. For once she didn't feel the need to chat nineteen to the dozen. Instead, she found that by watching Tony's movements and body language, she understood exactly what sort of day he'd had. She understood him completely.

She was clearing away the dishes when the doorbell chimed. It was Pam, her next door neighbour and good friend. As ever she looked smart in her business suit and heels.

Carol smiled. "Hi! You must have smelt the coffee."

"I could do with one, believe me," said Pam waltzing into the lounge and sitting down beside Tony on the sofa.

"Two minutes earlier, Pam, and you could have had a bite of my lamb chop," Tony joked.

"You're so sweet. You can share my apple turnover any time," said Pam crossing her legs.

Carol ignored their normal harmless banter. Tony and Pam had always got on well and while it could have been a stumbling block to a more jealous type than herself, Carol saw it as perfectly harmless fun. She trusted her husband and her friend completely.

Yet, for the first time she noticed that Pam's legs were crossed towards Tony.

"I need a man!" Pam declared, and Carol's mouth dropped open. Pam went on. "Someone bold and fearless."

"What's wrong with your own man?" Carol heard herself say, a little too sharply.

"He's still up North on business," Pam reminded her. "And I need one upstairs, right now!"

Tony sat on the edge of the sofa, looking keen and alert, and Carol found herself wondering why he had to look so eager. It was perfectly obvious that Pam wanted a fuse mending or a light bulb changing.

"Blown another fuse?" Carol asked, wishing Tony wouldn't sit there with his hands splayed over his thighs, as if he was about to leap up and save her life. That particular stance, according to her Body Language book meant he was ready, willing and able. But to do what exactly, Carol couldn't help but wonder.

"There's this monstrous spider in my bath," Pam explained with a shudder.

"Just turn the taps on," Carol suggested, a little too quickly. Aware that she was acting like someone with a jealous streak.

"Oh! I couldn't bear to watch it wriggling," Pam grimaced. "If Tony could just throw it out of the window, or something..."

"Oh, I'm sure Tony is capable of that," Carol answered, feeling awful for allowing herself to be jealous, over nothing. "I'll make that coffee."

Adding milk and one sugar, exactly how Pam liked hers, Carol reminded herself that Pam was her best friend, had been for years, and Tony had never been unfaithful in all their years of married life. She was certain of that.

After convincing herself that all was well, she took the tray of coffee back into the lounge. She almost dropped the lot when she noticed that Pam was, according to the book, displaying the most classic gesture of body language of when a woman was interested in a man.

She was sliding her foot in and out of her shoe as they chatted.

To the uninitiated, Pam's action would have meant nothing. But Carol had read that book from cover to cover, and if a woman was interested in a man, she would slip her foot in and out of her shoe. And should the shoe actually come off...!

Carol served the coffee, the smile on her face fixed and frozen. A minute later she almost choked, as Pam's shiny patent leather shoe slipped right off her foot.

Tony leapt up and patted his wife's back as Carol coughed and spluttered. "Gone down the wrong way, has it, love?"

"I'm all right," she said, her eyes fixed on Pam who was putting her shoe back on. She remained with her legs still crossed towards Tony when he sat back down.

When they'd finished their coffee, Tony rubbed his hands together. "Well, let's get this eight legged monster dealt with shall we?"

Pam jumped up. "My hero!"

Carol felt physically ill as she watched them both disappear next door. She grabbed her Body Language book from the shelf and swiftly thumbed through the pages, checking the facts.

There was no doubt about it. Tony and Pam were definitely attracted to each other.

Well, she wasn't about to stand by and let it happen. She dashed around to her neighbour's house. The front door was ajar and she tiptoed in, her heart hammering and her imagination running riot.

Tony appeared at the top of the stairs, just as Pam emerged from the kitchen and came slopping down the hall in her flip flops.

"He certainly was a big one!" said Tony. "Come to give me a hand, Carol love? I almost needed it, it was huge!"

"Told you!" said Pam giving Carol a quick hug. "Your husband is an absolute angel. I've been on my feet all day in those damn new shoes and my feet are killing me. If I don't get a good soak in the bath soon, I'll die."

Carol bit her lip, holding back the little splutter of relieved laughter. Sore feet! Pam had sore feet, she wasn't trying to lure her husband at all.

Back home, Carol closed the door on the evening air and turned towards Tony.

He was standing there, watching her, thumbs tucked through his belt. His usual stance, she realised. "Well, I fancy a nice lazy night in front of the fire," he said, smiling. "Wouldn't mind a bit of a read. What's that book you've been engrossed in all week?"

"Oh that. It's all about body language," Carol said, slipping her arms around her husband's neck. "I'm taking it back to the library tomorrow. Load of rubbish. Anyway, you don't need a book to understand my body language, do you?"

May Contain Nuts

by Margaret Mather

I'm sitting in the summer house with my air rifle across my legs. My wife has just brought me a cup of tea and a chocolate biscuit. She shakes her head at the sight of me, tells me I look like Elmer Fudd. I don't think I do, he never wore a red Ferrari baseball hat. And it was rabbits he didn't like.

My dislike is squirrels or one squirrel in particular. Every time I put nuts out for the birds, he's all over them like a rash. They disappear in a couple of hours. It's a matter of pride now. I will find him and I will, make him leave.

I've spent hours hatching plans to capture him, building new contraptions, watching them fail. My head hurts and my thinking has become illogical. My wife doesn't understand the frustration I feel. She says, 'live with it.'

She's a writer, my wife, and clueless about the real world. She lives inside her stories, where conflict is overcome by love or some other stupid emotion. It's not like that I keep telling her, but she never listens to me. The only thing left for me to do is to use my gun.

No, please don't worry, I don't mean on myself. I'm not ready to go yet and although my patience is being tried to the limit, that would be the last thing on my mind. Before you get the wrong end of the stick, I'm only going to pull the trigger, there will be no pellets in it but the noise should scare him.

"Clear off," I shout as loud as I can, trying to move him on.

Big brown eyes shrouded with heavy eyebrows stare back at me. He swings on the bird feeder using only one leg and his tail to balance. He seems to be egging me on, trying my patience to the limit.

"If you don't leave now, I won't be responsible for my actions," I say, my voice quivering with frustration.

Nothing, no response, just a look that says, 'do your worst.' I place the butt of the rifle to my shoulder, take careful aim then pull the trigger. The gun makes a dull clicking noise and the squirrel drops to the ground and scampers away.

It's time to call in my O.G.G.O. friends. They might have had similar experiences and be willing to share them. O.G.G.O. stands for Old Gits Going Out Club and was started by myself and two friends. There's still only the three of us in it and we like to plan trips to National Trust places around the country, ending at the nearest pub.

Brian is the chairman and event's organiser. He always looks neat and tidy. The creases in his jeans are razor sharp. He works out the route and is always the driver so unfortunately for him there is no beer involved when we stop at the pub.

Then there's Colin, he knows all there is to know about everything. He takes it upon himself to keep us fully informed of the history of any National Trust place that we visit. He does this on the journey there, which leaves few surprises.

I'm Bob and I just go along for the ride. Today they have agreed to come to my home and discuss squirrel avoidance tactics.

We all decide that our brain-storming would be enhanced with a few cans of beer and some sandwiches. The beer works quickly and our ideas become more outlandish.

"Let's put pellets in the gun. Have some fun," says Colin waving his tuna sandwich precariously in the air.

"My goodness, Colin, you sure know how to rock and roll," says Brian frantically trying to mop some spilt beer from his jeans.

We line the empty beer cans up at the bottom of the garden and take turns to fire. Shouts of stick your hands up and make my day - punk fill the air. After two hours of target practice, we are no nearer to a satisfactory solution. And now the other two have dozed off and I'm still trying to think of a way to rid myself of that pesky squirrel.

I must have joined my friends in slumber and awake with a start.

"Put the gun down and put your hands in the air."

What on earth is happening? Why are the police in my garden? Why are armed police in my garden? Where are my friends?

As I'm led away by two policemen, I glimpse the squirrel out of the corner of my eye. He's running back and forth over the summerhouse roof then he stops, turns and waves – yes waves at me. It almost looks like a victory salute.

I lift my head, make eye contact with him and mouth the words, I'll be back.

Playground Duty

by Mary Ogilvie

Like bees round a honey pot
Soft little hands
Pull, clutch, fondle, find
Their way to attention.

Faces cheeky with specks of food
Look up with adventure
Ready to start
Like the dawn of day.

Feet weighed down by leather
Trail shoelaces
Dangling, threatening
Ever ready to disobey.

Games, 'You are it'
'Catch me if you can'
Figures wandering in between
Or kicking a ball about.

Sobbing victims arrive
Displaying grazes on knees
Or bumps being exposed
To be comforted by soothing hands.

Crisps are the nicest
Different flavours, shapes and sizes
Munched by short sharp teeth
In little mouths.

Secluded from adult eyes
Conkers from a tree out of bounds
Hands searching
Through short wet grass.

Walking, checking, smiling
All is calm
Turning, shouting, running
Is there danger about?

'Granny is coming to tea'
'My tooth is nearly out'
A hand finds its way and cocoons
As we walk and talk.

A child looks anguished
Faces confronted
As words topple out
And spite and disorder are called to obey.

The whistle blows
Playtime over
Everything forgotten
Until a brand-new day.

_____

Welcome Home

by Mary Ogilvie

Two eyes see you walking down the street
Two ears hear the very footsteps as we meet
Two arms enfold you
Two tears come trickling down
Two words are spoken
So glad that you are found

An Edwardian Photograph

by Jonathan Robinson

"Watch the birdie just once more –
I know this must be a dreadful bore.
Smile – 'Say Cheese!' – let go the cat's tail!"
Begged Uncle Fred, his face set and pale.
The twins, both smirking for pure joy of life
Knew they were causing photographer's strife.
"Smile – Oh wipe your nose properly Marmaduke,
please!"
Soon he felt he would drop to his knees.
Up jumped Elizabeth, while mother so proud
Told Uncle off – "Don't shout quite so loud!
I don't like you yelling at my little dears,
The darlings are both blessed with delicate ears!
Preening herself, she said "They're like me."
Fred shut his mouth and counted to three.
Peered through the lens – his final attempt –
His face drawn and quartered, his hair now unkempt.
Click! Went the shutter; Fred kept to his silence
As he let his mind wander on small forms of violence.
Alas! The twins moved as the photo was blurred.
Where Fred ran off to, no man ever heard!

Cornered

It was a smile lighting the darkest corner, a laugh inviting adventure that vanished in a flash. They turned expecting exuberant banter; found Silence.

"Where's the Word?"
"Speechless"
"How?"
"Blocked, blanked, billed."
"And the Grin?"
"Frowned, furrowed, fallow."
"That chuckle?"
"Strangled, stamped, stumped"

The space went cold; chill spreading, guts tightening, tears swelling. They paused expecting a lonely empty door and found Delight.

"Whoop!, whoop!" giggled Glee.
"Yahoo!" chuckled Titter.
"LOL" texted Tone.
"Who? What? Why?" cried Censor.
"Mirth conquers melancholy" squealed Grin.
"Joy trumps dejection" cracked Ribs.
"Hilarity frees disharmony" beamed Word.

Smiling, their world turns a corner.

The Coventry Shout!

by Val Smith

You who can boast of your birth in this city
Should let the world know
of your long and proud past,
Your history of poverty, hard graft and learning
New skills, which has always been what you do best.
In times long ago success came to Coventry,
Rich Guilds, skilled craftsmen,
Lord Mayors and Aldermen,
And those world-famous Mystery Plays,
All showed new prosperity, crafts, skills and arts,
While villagers, nowadays powerful and rich,
Still dug crop patches in neighbouring Brum.
All English children know Coventry's history,
Eager to hear as their teachers narrate
The story of beautiful Lady Godiva,
Forced by her husband, the wicked Lord Leofric,
To ride "clothed in chastity", naked and cold,
Through crowds awed and silent,
eyes reverently closed,
Except for the villain, the first Peeping Tom,
Blind from that moment, punished by God!
A duel was once planned here,
and huge crowds assembled
Eyeing Kings, Queens,
and Nobles in our famous old city,
So famous indeed that throughout all of England
'Sent to Coventry' meant cut off
from right-thinking folk.
But not only the nobles made Coventry great!
The envious Germans tried to wipe out our city,
'Coventrated' old houses and our glorious cathedral.
So we built another! so splendid, so modern,

It fronted newspapers all over the world!
And wealth was created by talented citizens,
Which as one trade lost place in the stalls of the world
Had to turn to another,
and our young learnt new skills.
Watches and sewing-machines, bicycles, cars,
Lost their place in world trade.
So we tackled new skills, those internet mysteries–
Because nothing can fell you, you Coventry folk!!
So be proud, you Coventrians,
We're the best, the most versatile!
Don't doff your caps to
your 'nouveaux riches' neighbours,
But shout out our pride! Shout and shout loud!
We have plenty to shout about! Shout it! Out loud!

About the Authors

Margaret Egrot

Margaret Egrot is a playwright, novelist and blogger. Since 2015 she has published two YA novels and several short stories for teenagers and adults. Her latest book, CAST OFF, a collection of thirteen stories based on plays by Shakespeare, was released by Solstice Publishing in 2017.

Social Media links

Amazon author page: http://www.amazon.co.uk/-/e/B00RVO1BHO

Facebook: **facebook.com/pages/Margaret-Egrot/1374506486178952**

Twitter: **https://twitter.com/meegrot**

Blog: www.writingandbreathing.wordpress.com

John Sutton

I'm John Sutton, and I've had two of my short stories published now (including the one in here). Most of my efforts are rather longer, mind you...

Charles Satchwell

Charles Satchwell was born in Coventry and has been a metallurgist, teacher and soccer coach as well as working at many other jobs. He started writing for fun 10 years ago after attending a creative writing course. Completing a novel writing course at Warwick University gave him the tools to write his first novel, 'Brothers Lost.'

Beverley Woodley

Beverley Woodley works part-time in a library and full-time at becoming a writer. Her writing successfully won her a place at the 2016 WriteNow Birmingham event organised by Penguin Random House. This is her first published short story.

Owen Jennings
Creator of 'Play in a bag' Where all the props fit in one bag and can be carried to a venue. Members of the audience impromptu become the cast of the drama.

Sean Langley
Sean Langley is a Yorkshireman by birth, grew up in the south of England, and moved to Coventry in 2004. He writes slowly, for those that cannot read very quickly. Find out more at www.seanlangley.co.uk

Gwydion Williams
Gwydion M. Williams is the youngest son of writer and thinker Raymond Williams. Born in Sussex, he has lived in both Cambridgeshire and London. He went to university at Bangor North Wales, with a degree in Zoology. He worked as a computer analyst in the commercial sector: for the Norwich & Peterborough Building Society for his last 20 years. He was then living in Peterborough, but moved to Coventry when he retired. (His elder brother lives nearby in Kenilworth.)
He has written much, though little of it has been published. His main published work was in 2000, *Adam Smith: Wealth Without Nations'*, a left-wing but not exactly Marxist criticism of the work. It disputes that there is any rational basis for the claim that markets are self-regulating, and would not just be of interest to committed leftists.
He is currently working on an SF novel and another Fantasy novel, neither yet finished. You can find more about him at his website,
https://gwydionmadawc.com/about/

Hilary Hopker

Hilary works in communications for a large police force and is often inspired to write about crime and vulnerable people. She writes short stories, flash fiction, poetry and theatre reviews. She has won several writing prizes, been long and shortlisted in regional and national competitions and been published in national magazines and anthologies.

Emilie Lauren Jones

Emilie Lauren Jones is a performance poet and published writer of short stories, flash and microfiction.
Her first poem published was in Chatterbox Magazine when she was aged nine!
Emilie enjoys performing at events and festivals as well as delivering writing workshops. Her flash fiction series 'Fragment' is available to read on the American publishing website 'Chanillo.' Her book 'Sitting on the Pier' is available to order from Amazon and Waterstones.

David Court

David Court is a short story author and novelist, whose works have appeared in over a dozen venues including Tales to Terrify, Strangely Funny, Fears Accomplice and The Voices Within. Whilst primarily a horror writer, he also writes science fiction, poetry and satire.
His writing style has been described as "Darkly cynical" and "Quirky and highly readable" and David can't bring himself to disagree with either of those statements.
Growing up in the UK in the eighties, David's earliest influences were the books of Stephen King and Clive Barker, and the films of John Carpenter and George Romero. The first wave of Video Nasties may also

have had a profound effect on his psyche.

As well as writing, David works as a Software Developer and lives in Coventry with his wife, three cats and an ever-growing beard. David's wife once asked him if he'd write about how great she was. David replied that he would, because he specialized in short fiction. Despite that, they are still married.

You can find out more about David at www.davidjcourt.co.uk.

Ann Evans

Ann Evans was born and bred in Coventry, and started writing just for fun after giving up her secretarial job to have her three children.

Having caught the writing 'bug' there was no stopping her, and as her children grew up, she continued to write for all kinds of genres, from compiling and editing her parish magazine, to writing school pantomimes. She then got a job at her local newspaper, sneaking in through the back door, as she puts it, to become a staff feature writer.

She is now a full time freelance writer, writing magazine articles on a wide range of topics, plus writing adventure and mystery books for children, young adults, reluctant readers, romance and adult crime. To date she has 29 books to her name and more in the pipeline.

She is a member of the Romantic Novelists Association, The Society of Women Writers and Journalists and the National Association of Writers in Education. She is also a Patron of Reading for a Coventry senior school.

Www.annevansbooks.co.uk

Mary Ogilvie

Since becoming a member of Coventry Writers' Group, I have learnt much about the craft of writing. Being with like-minded people has been both helpful and inspiring. Poetry, short stories, articles, play writing and being a Grassroot reporter for the local newspaper have come from my pen. Over the years I've had a variety of different items published in magazines and newspapers. I continue to learn.

Jonathan Robinson

This will be the third poem Jonathan has had published in an anthology. He has had a novel drafted for about twenty years and feels sure one day it will publish itself. He much prefers writing poems as they are generally shorter than prose.
Jonathan has a HND in Illustration from Carmarthen College of Technology and Arts, Wales, but has only recently found time to return to his loves of poetry writing and drawing.
Jonathan drives a forklift at work and finds it safer not to daydream about poetry whilst doing so.

Margaret Mather

Margaret writes articles, short stories and poems. She's had articles published in many magazines including Landscape,Yours,Irelands Own,Scottish Memories, Best of British and Classic Bus.She is a member of the SWWJ and is delighted to have a story in this anthology.

Craig Muir

Craig Muir is a minister of the United Reformed Church who writes poems, played with words and is trying out flash fiction, often based on the everyday stories people share with him. You can find more at http://speechless.blogspirit.com.

Printed in Great Britain
by Amazon